Health Science Projects About Psychology

Robert Gardner
and
Barbara Gardner Conklin

Science Projects

Enslow Publishers, Inc.

40 Industrial Road	PO Box 38
Box 398	Aldershot
Berkeley Heights, NJ 07922	Hants GU12 6BP
USA	UK

http://www.enslow.com

In memory of Natalie S. Gardner
Loving wife and mother

Library of Congress Cataloging-in-Publication Data

Gardner, Robert, 1929–
  Health science projects about psychology / Robert Gardner and
Barbara Gardner Conklin.
      p. cm. — (Science projects)
      Includes bibliographical references and index.
      Summary: Uses science projects to explore such areas of psychology as personality,
emotions, perception, learning, memory, and parapsychology.
      ISBN 0-7660-1439-8
      1. Psychology—Experiments—Juvenile literature. 2. Psychology, Experimental—
Juvenile literature. [1. Psychology—Experiments. 2. Experiments. 3. Science projects.]
  I. Conklin, Barbara Gardner. II. Title.
  BF198.7 .G37   2002
  150'.78—dc21
                                                          2001003425

Printed in the United States of America

10 9 8 7 6 5 4 3 2 1

To Our Readers:
We have done our best to make sure all Internet addresses in this book were active and
appropriate when we went to press. However, the author and the publisher have no control
over and assume no liability for the material available on those Internet sites or on other Web
sites they may link to. Any comments or suggestions can be sent by e-mail to
comments@enslow.com or to the address on the back cover.

Illustration credits: Stephen F. Delisle

Cover illustration: Jerry McCrea(foreground); © Corel Corporation
(background).

Contents

*appropriate ideas for science fair project

*appropriate ideas for science fair project

Introduction

The science projects and experiments in this book have to do with psychology—that is, with the mental, emotional, and learning behavior of humans and other animals. You can learn a lot about psychology by doing experiments. Most of the materials you will need for carrying out your investigations can be found in your home.

For some of the experiments you will need a number of people to help you by serving as subjects. Be sure that your experiments do not in any way injure, insult, or cause mental distress to those who volunteer to serve as subjects.

Like all good scientists, you will find it useful to record in a notebook your ideas, notes, data, and anything you can conclude from your experiments. By so doing, you can keep track of the information you gather and the conclusions you reach. Using your notebook, you can refer to experiments you have done, which may help you with future projects. In some of the experiments you will have to make some calculations to analyze the data you collect. Therefore, you may find it helpful to have a calculator nearby.

Science Fairs

Some of the projects in this book may be appropriate for a science fair. They are indicated by an asterisk (*). However, judges at such fairs do not reward projects or experiments that are simply copied from a book. For example, a model of the human eye, which is commonly found at these fairs, would probably not impress judges unless it was done in a novel or creative way. A model of the eye with a flexible lens that could produce images that explain common illusions would receive more consideration than a rigid papier-mâché model.

Science fair judges tend to reward creative thought and imagination. It is difficult to be creative or imaginative unless you are really interested in your project. Therefore, be sure to choose a subject that appeals to you. Before you jump into a project, consider, too, your own talents and the cost of materials you will need.

If you decide to use a project found in this book for a science fair, you should find ways to modify or extend it. This should not be difficult, because you will probably discover that as you carry out these investigations new ideas for experiments will come to mind—experiments that could make excellent science fair projects, particularly because the ideas are your own and are interesting to you.

If you decide to enter a science fair and have never done so before, you should read some of the books listed in the Further Reading section, as well as *Science Fair Projects—Planning, Presenting, Succeeding*, which is one of the books in this series. These books deal specifically with science fairs and will provide plenty of helpful hints and lots of useful information that will enable you to avoid the pitfalls that sometimes plague first-time entrants. You will learn how to prepare appealing reports that include charts and graphs, how to set up and display your work, how to present your project, and how to relate to judges and visitors.

Safety First

Most of the projects included in this book are perfectly safe. However, the following safety rules are well worth reading before you start any project.

1. Do any experiments or projects, whether from this book or of your own design, under the supervision of a science teacher or other knowledgeable adult.

2. Read all instructions carefully before proceeding with a project. If you have questions, check with your supervisor before going any further.

3. Maintain a serious attitude while conducting experiments. Fooling around can be dangerous to you and to others.

4. Do not eat or drink while experimenting.

1

Early Experiments in Psychology

The word *psychology* is derived from the Greek word *psyche*, which means "soul." But *psychology* has come to mean "the study of the behavior of humans and other animals." Human behavior is difficult to understand because it involves both biology and social interactions. Psychology is therefore regarded as a biosocial science.

The human nervous system responds to stimuli, outside agents that create an action. For instance, a crack of thunder causes our ears to hear. However, what we sense and the way we respond are influenced by the setting in which we grew up. Scientists have been experimenting for more than 150 years to unlock the secrets of the human mind.

The first psychology experiments were conducted by physiologists, scientists who study life processes. Physiologists were trying to measure, or estimate, the speed at which nerve impulses travel in the human body. By measuring reaction time—the time it takes for a person to respond to an outside agent—they could estimate the time it takes an impulse to travel from the eye to the back of the brain and then to the hand.

In Experiment 1-3 you will discover, as did nineteenth-century scientists, that we are limited in our ability to distinguish the intensity of one stimulus from another.

1-1*
Reaction Time

You can carry out an experiment like the first ones done by psychologists. It will measure a human's reaction time: the speed of response to an outside stimulus.

Things you will need:

• yardstick
• Table 1
• a friend

First, find a smooth wall that will not be harmed by a few fingerprints, perhaps in the kitchen. Place a yardstick against the wall with the zero end down. Stand to one side of the yardstick and place one thumb against the yardstick at about the ten-inch mark, as shown in Figure 1. Keep the rest of your hand flat against the wall.

Ask your subject to stand in front of the yardstick with her preferred hand flat against the wall, thumb raised slightly above the yardstick's surface just below the 2-inch mark. The subject can stop the fall of the yardstick by moving her thumb quickly toward the wall.

To begin the experiment, say to the subject, "Watch my thumb, which is pressing the yardstick against the wall. When I move that thumb up to release the yardstick, move your thumb against the yardstick and stop its fall. A few seconds before I release the yardstick, I will say, 'Get ready.' At that point, watch my thumb closely. When you see it move, move your thumb as quickly as you can to stop the yardstick. Then wait for me to record the distance it fell."

Repeat the experiment five times. Each time wait between one and five seconds after you say "Get ready" before raising your thumb to release the yardstick so that the subject cannot anticipate the release. If the subject does try to anticipate your release, start over; that is, do five more trials.

Record the distance the yardstick falls after each trial by subtracting 2 inches (the initial position of the subject's thumb) from the number of inches (including fractions) just above the final

11

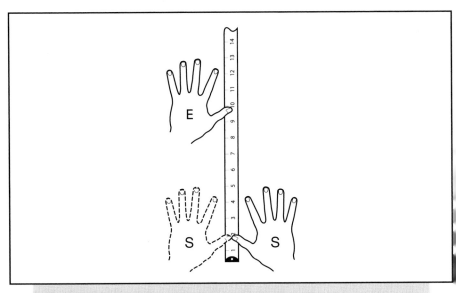

Figure 1. This drawing shows the ruler and the position of the hands of the experimenter (E) and subject (S). The drawing assumes the subject is right-handed. Left-handed subjects should use their left hands. The dotted lines show the position of the left hand of a right-handed subject during the second part of the experiment.

position of the subject's thumb. Then calculate the average distance it fell over the five trials. On Table 1, you can use the average distance the yardstick fell to find the subject's reaction time.

What reaction time will you record in your notebook if the yardstick fell 11 inches?

What reaction time should you record if the yardstick fell 20 ½ inches?

Repeat the entire experiment, but this time you will be the subject and your subject will be the experimenter.

Based on the results of both experiments, estimate, in inches per second, the speed at which nerve impulses travel in the human body. After completing the next two parts of this experiment, you will have enough data to make an analysis and draw some conclusions about reaction time.

Table 1. The right-hand column in the table shows the time for an object to fall each of the distances shown in the left-hand column. The subject's reaction time is the time in the right-hand column. Times have been rounded to the nearest hundredths of a second. (Note the abbreviations: in = inches; s = seconds.)

Distance the yardstick fell (in)	Time to fall this distance; Reaction time (s)
1.0	0.07
2.0	0.10
3.0	0.13
4.0	0.14
5.0	0.16
6.0	0.18
8.0	0.20
10.0	0.23
12.0	0.25
14.0	0.27
16.0	0.29
18.0	0.31
20.0	0.32
22.0	0.34
24.0	0.35
28.0	0.38
32.0	0.41
36.0	0.43

Reaction Time Involving Discrimination

In the second part of this experiment, the subject must discriminate—make a judgment—between two stimuli. In releasing the yardstick, you, as the experimenter, will lift either your thumb or your index finger. If you raise your index finger, the yardstick will not fall. If you raise your thumb, the yardstick will fall as it did in the first part of this experiment. The subject will now have to watch both your thumb and index finger and make a decision based on the two stimuli presented.

Record the distance the yardstick falls after each trial in which you lift your thumb. (Obviously, there can be no determination of reaction time if the yardstick does not fall.) Calculate the average distance it fell over five trials. Use Table 1, as before, to determine the subject's reaction time.

Switch roles with your subject and repeat the second part of the experiment.

Reaction Time Involving a Choice

In the third part of this experiment, the subject has to make a choice between two responses. In releasing the yardstick, you will either lift your thumb straight toward the subject or move it toward your index finger as you raise it. The subject will now have both thumbs raised just below the 2-inch mark (as shown by the dotted-line hand and the solid-line hand in Figure 1).

Tell your subject to use her left thumb to stop the yardstick when your thumb is raised toward her and her right thumb to stop the yardstick when you move your thumb toward your index finger.

Again, repeat the experiment five times and record the distance the yardstick falls after each trial. (If the subject uses the wrong thumb, start over; that is, do five more trials.) Then calculate the average distance the yardstick fell over the five valid trials. Using Table 1, determine the subject's average reaction time.

Switch roles with your subject and repeat the third part of this experiment.

How do the reaction times for the first, second, and third parts of the experiment compare? Is there any significant difference in reaction time if the subject has to discriminate between two different stimuli as in the second part of the experiment? Is there any significant difference in reaction time if the subject has to make a choice between responses as in the third part of the experiment? If there are differences in reaction time under these three conditions, can you explain what the cause might be?

Exploring on Your Own

Repeat this experiment with a number of different subjects. Does reaction time seem to be related to a subject's age? To a subject's gender? To a subject's athletic ability?

Design and conduct an experiment to test reaction time when a subject has to discriminate among three stimuli. Design another experiment to test reaction time when a subject has to choose among three responses to three different stimuli. How does the number of alternative stimuli or responses affect the reaction time?

1-2*
Reaction Time Using Sound as a Stimulus

Repeat the first part of Experiment 1-1 using a sound stimulus in place of a visual stimulus. Have the subject close her eyes or blindfold her and tell her that

Things you will need:
- yardstick
- Table 1
- a friend

you will say "Go!" at the moment you release the yardstick. Upon hearing this sound stimulus, the subject is to react as before and move her thumb as quickly as possible to stop the yardstick. Repeat the experiment five times. For each trial, record the distance the yardstick falls. Then determine the average distance the yardstick fell and use Table 1 to determine the subject's average reaction time.

How does the reaction time to a sound stimulus compare to the reaction time for the visual stimulus you used in the first part of Experiment 1-1? Are they significantly different? That is, do they consistently differ by more than 0.05 to 0.1 seconds? If they do, can you explain?

Exploring on Your Own

Design an experiment to measure the reaction time to a touch stimulus. How does it compare with the reaction times to sound and to visual stimuli?

16

1-3
What Difference in Weight Is Noticeable?

Another early experiment in human psychology involved distinguishing a change in the intensity of a weight stimulus: in other words, deciding whether one object is heavier than another. You can do a very simple experiment to see how deceiving a weight stimulus can be. Find a very large can and a very small can. Add sand to the small can until its weight is the same as that of the large empty can. Now ask someone to lift both cans, one at a time. Which can do they think is heavier? Can you explain why they think one can is heavier than the other?

Things you will need:

• very large can and very small can

• sand

• balance or scale

• several people to serve as subjects

• notebook

• pen or pencil

• blindfold

• table

• chair

• standard weights found in most science labs: 10 to 200 grams (g) in 10-g increments; 300 to 2,000 g in 100-g increments; and 50 g weight

• watch or clock with second hand

Next, test people to find the "just noticeable difference" in weight that they can detect. To do this, blindfold a subject seated at a table. Ask the subject to keep his elbow on the table as he lifts a 100-gram weight, the handle of which you place between his thumb and first two fingers. The 100-gram weight will serve as the standard. Have the subject lift the standard. Then, after a five-second wait, have him lift a second weight for comparison. For comparison weights use 10, 20, 30, 40, 50, 60, 70, 80, 90, 110, 120, 130, 140, 150, 160, 170, 180, 190, and 200 grams (g). After the second in each pair of lifts, ask the subject whether the second weight is lighter, heavier, or the same weight as the standard. Record each response and the comparison weight.

What is the smallest difference in weight the subject can detect? Is it the same for weights greater than 100 g as it is for weights less than 100 g?

Now repeat the experiment using 1,000 g (1 kg) as the standard weight. For comparison weights, use 100, 200, 300, 400, 500, 600, 700, 800, 900, 950, 1,050, 1,100, 1,200, 1,300, 1,400, 1,500, 1,600, 1,700, 1,800, 1,900, and 2,000 grams.

Record each response and the comparison weight. What is the smallest difference in weight the subject can detect? Is it the same for weights greater than 1,000 g as it is for weights less than 1,000 g?

How does the just noticeable difference for the heavier weights compare with the just noticeable difference for the lighter weights? How does the ratio of the just noticeable difference to the standard weight compare for the 100 g and the 1,000 g standard weights? Can you reach any conclusions regarding these differences?

Animals and Psychology

For many experiments, early psychologists found it convenient to use animals rather than humans. Present-day psychologists, as well, often do experiments with animals. Sometimes understanding the behavior of animals helps to explain human behavior. Sometimes it simply leads to a better understanding of animal behavior.

In their natural habitat, the male three-spined stickleback (a species of fish) exhibits a unique behavior pattern during the mating season. He constructs a nest and then induces the female to lay her eggs there by doing an elaborate dance. But what triggers such behavior in the male stickleback?

To find out, scientists constructed a variety of models of the female stickleback and placed them near a male. They tried moving the female fish model in various ways and had the model approach the male in different ways. The only stimulus that caused the male to begin his elaborate behavior was to present a model in which the female's abdomen was swollen. The experiment revealed that it was an egg-swollen abdomen that induced the male to begin his ritualistic behavior.

Can animals solve problems that require thinking? It looks that way. If a chimpanzee is unable to reach a piece of fruit outside his cage with either of two sticks that fit together, he will join the two sticks to make one long enough to pull the fruit to within his reach.

1-4*
The Behavior of Mealworms

Like many insects, the grain beetle *(Tenebrio molitor)* passes through four distinct stages in its life cycle, as shown in Figure 2. Mealworms are the larval stage of this beetle. The larval stage lasts about four months. The mealworm then goes into a resting (pupal) stage for about two weeks before the adult beetles emerge. The adults live for several months, and each female will lay about 500 eggs before she dies. These eggs hatch into mealworms in about a week. Mealworms are useful for experiments because their eggs hatch quickly, they are inexpensive, and they are easy to care for.

For your experiments, you will need several dozen mealworms. You can buy them from a local pet store or from a biological supply house. The worms will live nicely in a small glass, plastic, or metal container (see Figure 3). Put a handful of bran or dry cereal, such as bran flakes, corn flakes, or wheat flakes, into the container. Cover

Things you will need:
- mealworms (several dozen) obtained from a local pet store
- small glass, plastic, or metal container
- bran or dry cereal, such as bran flakes, corn flakes, or wheat flakes
- paper towel
- potato or apple
- cardboard shoe box
- clear tape
- mirror, or a sheet of clear rigid plastic
- small glass jar
- refrigerator
- white paper
- magnifying glass
- ruler
- cardboard
- paper drinking straw
- table
- talcum powder
- flashlight
- cotton swabs
- vinegar
- ammonia water
- water
- pencil or toothpick
- paper of several different colors
- scissors
- paper with a pattern
- different surfaces such as shiny paper, silk, sandpaper, newspaper, felt, and wood

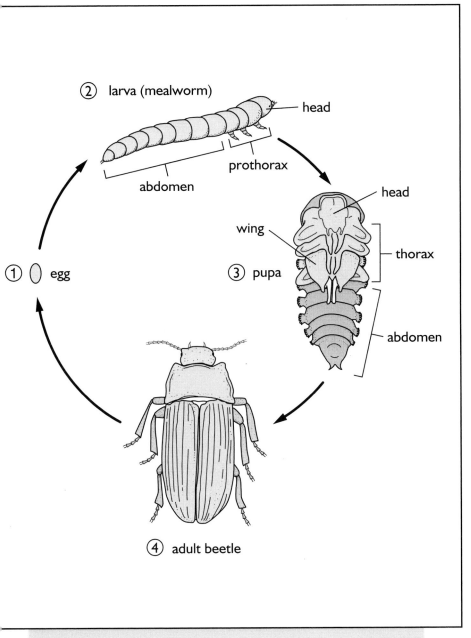

Figure 2. The life cycle of a mealworm (*Tenebrio molitor*). Drawings are about four times actual size.

the food with a paper towel. Put a piece of fresh potato or apple on the towel. The fresh food will provide all the water the mealworms need.

If you would like to watch the life cycle of these beetles, simply change the food supply when the bran or cereal flakes become powdery. Add fresh pieces of potato or apple occasionally to provide moisture.

General Behavior of Mealworms

Put about 20 of your mealworms in a cardboard shoe box. A strip of clear tape around the top edge of the box will cause them to slip back if they try to crawl out. Just watch the mealworms for a while. Notice their tendency to move along walls and around corners.

To see how mealworms move, place one on a mirror or a sheet of clear rigid plastic. How many legs does the mealworm have? How do the legs move as the animal walks? How fast does it walk? How long would it take a mealworm to walk a mile?

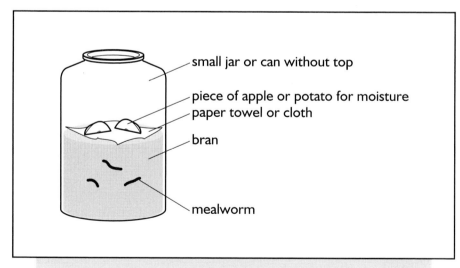

small jar or can without top

piece of apple or potato for moisture
paper towel or cloth

bran

mealworm

Figure 3. A place to keep and nurture mealworms.

Place one or two mealworms in a small glass jar. Put the jar in the refrigerator for a few minutes. The cold temperature will make the mealworms move more slowly, so they will be easier to observe. When the mealworms are sluggish, remove them from the refrigerator. Put them on a piece of white paper and examine them closely with a magnifying glass. How big are they? How wide? How many segments make up their bodies? Can you find their eyes? Their antennae? Their mouthparts? What do their legs look like? Do they have fine hairs on their body? If so, what might these be used for?

Place a mealworm at the center of a small sheet of cardboard. Raise one side of the cardboard so that the mealworm is on an inclined plane. Which way does the mealworm move? Repeat the experiment with the cardboard at different angles of incline. Does the mealworm always move the same way? Is the mealworm's movement affected by the angle of the incline?

Put a paper drinking straw on a table. Place a mealworm head-first into the drinking straw. What does the mealworm do? What happens if you place the mealworm into the straw tail first?

How Do Mealworms Find Food?

Try to discover how mealworms detect food. Do they see it, do they smell it, or do they just bump into it by accident? To find out, cover the bottom of the shoe box with a very fine layer of talcum powder. The worms will leave tracks in the powder when they move. Place a small pile of bran or dry cereal flakes near the center of the box. Then put about a dozen mealworms at one end of the box. After the worms have found the food, examine the paths they followed. How do you think they found the food? Do you think they would find the food sooner if you put the food near a wall?

How Can You Make a Mealworm Back Up?

Mealworms sometimes move backward. What stimuli might make a mealworm move backward? Here are a few to try. You may be able to think of some others. Try each stimulus many times with different mealworms.

- Shine a flashlight at the mealworm. If the worm backs up, is it because of the light or the flashlight itself? How can you find out?

- Dip a cotton swab into vinegar. Hold it in front of the mealworm. Repeat the experiment using ammonia water. Repeat once more with water.

- Touch the mealworm gently with a pencil or a toothpick. What happens? Does it matter where you touch the animal?

- Make a loud noise near the mealworm.

- Blow air through a drinking straw at the mealworm. What happens? Does it matter where the air hits the mealworm?

- Block a worm's path with different kinds of material.

Which stimulus works best? Is there any stimulus that works every time?

Do Mealworms Have a Favorite Color?

Put four papers of different color on the floor of a cardboard shoe box. Place a white paper circle in the center of the box, as shown in Figure 4. Put a few mealworms on the white circle. Do they seem to have a preference for one color? What evidence do you have?

Design an experiment to see if mealworms prefer paper with a pattern as opposed to plain paper.

Do mealworms have a preference with respect to the surface over which they crawl? You might try shiny paper, silk, sandpaper, newspaper, felt, and wood. What do you find?

Mealworms in Mazes

You can cut and bend cardboard to make walls inside a shoe box. Place the walls so as to make T-mazes, such as those shown in

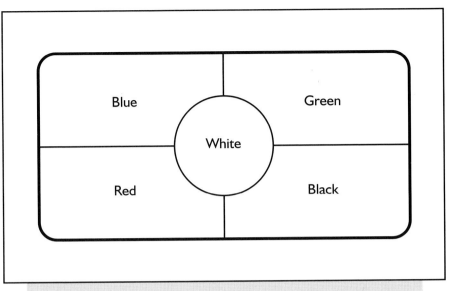

Figure 4. Do mealworms have a favorite color?

Figure 5. (Why do you think they are called T-mazes?) As you can see, the maze labeled A forces the worm to make a left turn in order to reach the food at the end of the maze. The maze labeled B forces the worm to make a right turn.

Does forcing a worm to turn right or left at the start of the maze affect the way it will turn (right or left) when given a choice at the end of the maze?

Does the length the worm has to crawl after the forced turn affect the direction it turns at the end of the maze?

Cleanup

You might like to keep mealworms and watch them go through the pupal and adult stages of their life cycle. At some point, you will want to dispose of the insects by placing them and their remaining food in a sealed bag that can be placed in the garbage.

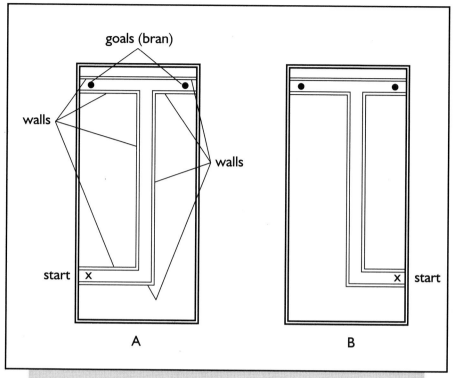

Figure 5. Mealworm mazes with forced turns.

Exploring on Your Own

Design experiments to find out how temperature, type of food, moisture, and other factors affect the length of the beetle's life cycle.

Design a variety of mealworm mazes. What can you learn about mealworm behavior from these mazes?

Design experiments to answer one or more of the following questions:

1. Can mealworms see?

2. Will mealworms crawl over the edge of a table and fall or will they stay along the table's edge?

3. Can mealworms hear?

4. Mealworms are often seen crawling along walls. How do they find a wall? How do they sense that the wall is there?

5. Do mealworms prefer light or darkness?

6. What food do mealworms like best?

7. Do mealworms prefer a dry or a moist environment?

2

Perception

At this moment you are being bombarded by stimuli—light from all the objects around you; sounds of voices, birds, or cars; and tastes, if you are eating. You smell odors, possibly of food, perfume, soap, or newly cut grass. You receive touch sensations from this book, the chair on which you sit, and the floor that presses against your feet. Despite all these stimuli, you are generally aware of only a few. If you are listening to music, you tend to ignore other stimuli. Your attention is on the sounds. You may even close your eyes to reduce light stimuli. If you are looking at a beautiful painting, light stimuli prevail; you may be unaware of the words spoken by those nearby.

You perceive something when you become consciously aware of it by using one or more of your senses to receive stimuli from it. It might be a sentence you are reading, a musical theme you are hearing, or the odor of a flower you are smelling.

The knowledge you acquire through your senses is called perception. However, as some of the experiments in this chapter will reveal, what you perceive is influenced by past experience. Furthermore, what you perceive may not be what it appears to be. The real world is often very different from the world you perceive.

2-1*
Perception of Temperature

There are sense receptors in your skin that respond to hot and cold. However, how you perceive temperature depends on the previous environment to which your sense receptors for temperature were exposed. This was first discovered by a German physiologist named Ernst Weber (1795–1878).

Things you will need:

• 3 large bowls

• tap water (hot and cold)

• ice cubes

• clock or watch

To begin this experiment, obtain three large bowls. To the first bowl add room-temperature tap water until the bowl is three-fourths full. Fill a second bowl about halfway with cold tap water. Add ice cubes until this bowl is also three-fourths full. Fill a third bowl to the same level with hot tap water. **As you add hot water to the bowl, test the water in the bowl with your hand. Be sure the water is not too hot. If it is, add some cold water until you are able to place your right hand in the water without discomfort.**

Place the three bowls side by side with the hot water on your right, the ice water on your left, and the room-temperature water in the middle. Dry your hands thoroughly. Then place your right hand in the hot water and your left hand in the ice water. Hold them under the water for three minutes.

After three minutes, remove your hands from the bowls and put both of them into the bowl of room-temperature water. How does your right hand perceive the water's temperature? How does your left hand perceive the water's temperature?

What does this experiment tell you about the way past experiences influence your perception of temperature?

Exploring on Your Own

Place a large wooden object and a large metallic object side by side in the same room for an hour so that you know both objects are at the same temperature. Now touch first one object and then the other. Why do you think you perceive their temperatures to be different?

2-2
Weber's Deception: Cold-Plus-Pressure Receptor Sensitivity

Ernst Weber, the man who discovered that temperature receptors are not good thermometers, gave his name to the effect you will see in this experiment. The experiment will show how temperature can affect a person's perception of weight.

Ask a friend to lie on his back on the floor with his eyes closed. Place on his forehead, to one side, a standard 20-gram metal weight (or a stack of six pennies glued together) that has been in warm (40°C, or 104°F) water for several minutes. On the other side of his forehead place an identical 20-gram metal weight (or stack of pennies) that has been resting on an ice cube for the same length of time. Does your subject perceive the two objects to be equal in mass? If not, which one does he think weighs more?

Try the same experiment with a number of subjects. Are your results always the same? Can you offer an explanation for the way the weights are perceived?

Things you will need:

- a friend
- two 20-gram standard metal weights or two stacks of 6 pennies glued together
- warm (40°C, or 104°F) water and cup
- ice cube
- several people

31

2-3*
Two Eyes Are Better than One

Normally, most people view the world with two eyes. We see a slightly different world with one eye than we do with the other. To see that this is true, lift your right arm and hold it straight out

Things you will need:
- a friend
- Ping-Pong ball
- 2 pencils
- ruler

to the side. Then close your left eye and stare straight ahead. How far do you have to move your right arm forward before you can see your right hand with your right eye?

Now close your right eye. How far do you have to move your right arm forward before you can see your right hand with your left eye?

Repeat the experiment using your left arm. Then repeat the experiment for both arms with both eyes open.

As you have seen, your right eye sees more on the right side of your visual field than does your left eye, and vice versa.

Depth Perception

A stereoscopic picture is made by taking two photographs of the same object at slightly different angles and then superimposing one on the other. Such a picture provides a sense of depth. Your eyes automatically provide a stereoscopic picture. The central part of an image falls on corresponding parts of the retinas of both eyes. Your right eye, as you have seen, sees more of an object on the right than does your left eye. Similarly, your left eye sees more of an object on the left than does your right eye. Your brain sees the central part of the image as a single image because the impulses come from corresponding parts of the two retinas. It then adds the extra parts seen only by the right and left eye to the central part to create an image that provides depth as well as breadth and height.

To compare your perception of depth using one eye and then two, try the following experiments. Begin by playing catch with a friend using a Ping-Pong ball. Do you find it easier to catch the ball when you use two eyes or one?

Next, ask your friend to hold a pencil about 30 cm (1 ft) in front of you about waist high. With both eyes open, try to touch the tip of the pencil with the tip of another pencil that you hold in your dominant hand. Now repeat the experiment with one eye closed. Then try the same experiment with the other eye closed. What evidence do you have that two eyes provide better depth perception than one?

As you have seen, viewing the world through two eyes helps you perceive depth. What other clues or stimuli do we use in perceiving a three-dimensional world?

Exploring on Your Own

Find out how filmmakers produce movies with three-dimensional effects. Why haven't such movies become popular?

Roll a sheet of paper into a tube. Look at a distant object with both eyes. Focus your attention so that you perceive just one small part of the object. Now hold the tube in front of one eye and again look at the same part of the distant object. Why do you think the tube improves your ability to perceive distant objects?

Perception: Constancy and Organization

Objects tend to be seen as constant even when the stimuli we receive from them are very different. You perceive a professional football player as a large man even though he is no more than several inches tall when viewed from the stands where you sit.

We also tend to organize our perceptions in ways that may be inborn. The genes that we inherit may program the way we perceive things.

Figure from Ground

We are generally able to distinguish the essential figure (object) or pattern we see from its background. For example, as you read these words, you do not focus on the white background of the paper but rather on the black print. There are exceptions. Camouflage is used, especially by the military and by nature, to avoid having a figure stand out from the surroundings. And there are reversible figures (see Figure 6a). Reversible figures are carefully designed to provide the brain with two options so that a figure can become the ground and vice versa.

Grouping

Gestalt psychologists believe many things can be perceived only in their entirety; that the whole is greater than the sum of its parts. They contend that we are born with a tendency to group objects on the basis of similarity, closeness, wholeness, and continuity. Objects similar in shape, size, or color tend to be grouped together (Figure 6b). Stimuli that arise from points close to one another tend to be perceived as belonging together (Figure 6c).

When we see part of an object, we often perceive the whole object. This, Gestalt psychologists say, reveals our tendency to "want" to see things as being whole even though in reality we are seeing only a part of the whole thing.

Similarly, lines that form only part of a figure tend to be seen as a complete figure (see Figure 6d). Motions, such as that of a car moving along a curved path, may be perceived as part of a whole, such as the car's moving in a circle. We expect objects moving along an arc to continue moving in that pattern and, therefore, to follow a circular path even though they may fly off along a tangent if we continue to follow the motion.

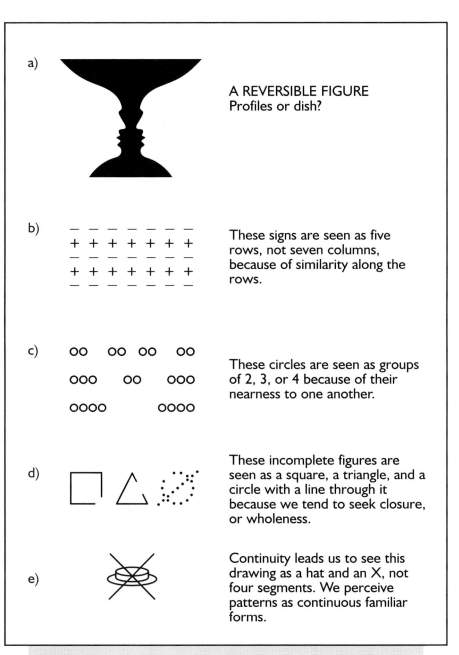

a)

A REVERSIBLE FIGURE
Profiles or dish?

b)

These signs are seen as five rows, not seven columns, because of similarity along the rows.

c)

These circles are seen as groups of 2, 3, or 4 because of their nearness to one another.

d)

These incomplete figures are seen as a square, a triangle, and a circle with a line through it because we tend to seek closure, or wholeness.

e)

Continuity leads us to see this drawing as a hat and an X, not four segments. We perceive patterns as continuous familiar forms.

Figure 6. Examples of a) reversibility, b) similarity, c) closeness, d) wholeness, and e) continuity.

2-4
Constancy, Figure-Ground, and Organization in Perceiving

Things you will need:

• Figures 6 and 7

• as many subjects as possible

• pencil

To illustrate constancy of perception, cover the caption in Figure 7 and ask a subject to look at the drawings of the door. Ask the subject, "What is the shape of the door in these drawings?" Most subjects will tell you the door has a rectangular shape. After they have answered your question, let them read the caption.

Cover the words beside Figure 6a and show it to as many subjects, one at a time, as possible. Do most people see both a pair of white facial profiles and a black dish? Can anyone see both at the same time?

See if you can design and draw one or more reversible figures of your own.

To illustrate the tendency of people to perceive similarity in shape, cover the words beside Figure 6b and show it to subjects. Ask them, "How would you describe these signs?" Most will probably see them in rows, but some will see columns.

The effect of proximity (closeness) in perception can be illustrated by using Figure 6c in the same way. Ask the subjects, "How many groups of circles do you see?" Most will perceive them as nine groups because of their proximity. They see groups of two (5), three (2), and four (2).

As another example of proximity, this time using sound stimuli, ask a subject to listen carefully. Then tap on a table twice in rapid succession. Wait a second and then tap twice again in rapid succession. Ask your subject how many taps he has heard. How does her response illustrate grouping according to closeness?

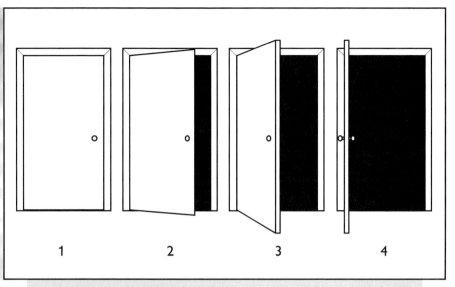

Figure 7. The image of the door in position is a rectangle on your retina. But as the door opens to positions 2 and 3 its image on your retina is a trapezoid. Yet you still perceive it to be a rectangle.

To illustrate the human tendency to perceive things as whole even though the stimuli may be incomplete, cover the words beside Figure 6d. Then ask a subject to tell you what he sees. Most will see a square, a triangle, and a circle with a line through it. Our tendency to perceive things as complete or whole is so strong that we usually ignore missing parts.

Finally, repeat the process with Figure 6e. Subjects will probably see a hat and an X, not four segments. We tend to perceive patterns that are continuous and familiar.

2-5*
Perception Constancy and Illusions

Figure 7 is an illustration of our tendency to perceive the materials that make up the world as being constant (unchanging). In a way, such a process makes life easier. If we had to continually pay close attention to the way we perceive common objects, we would have little time for more important activities.

Things you will need:

- Figures 7, 8, and 9
- index card
- table
- red, green, blue, yellow, cyan, magenta, and black paper squares that are about 10 cm (4 in) on a side
- 2 sheets of white paper

Design and prepare some drawings of your own that illustrate perception constancy.

Illusions are incorrect perceptions common to all who perceive the stimuli. In some cases our sense organs are simply responding to stimuli in a natural way. Other illusions are probably the result of past experience and the culture in which we live.

In some illusions the figure's orientation can switch because the brain can interpret either choice as having equal significance or likelihood. Examine the reversible figure illusions in Figure 8. Design some reversible image illusions of your own.

Without good depth perception, a person may see some structures in more than one equally likely orientation. You can see this for yourself. Take an index card and fold it in half along its long axis, as shown in Figure 9. Make the folded seam very sharp by applying pressure along it with your fingernail. Place the card on a table and stare at it with one eye closed. You will see that it can be seen as resting on its long edges or on its short edges. Your brain regards either orientation as equally possible. Why does the illusion disappear when you look at it with both eyes?

An illusion may be the result of sensory cell fatigue, when cells can no longer go on working correctly. To see such an illusion, place

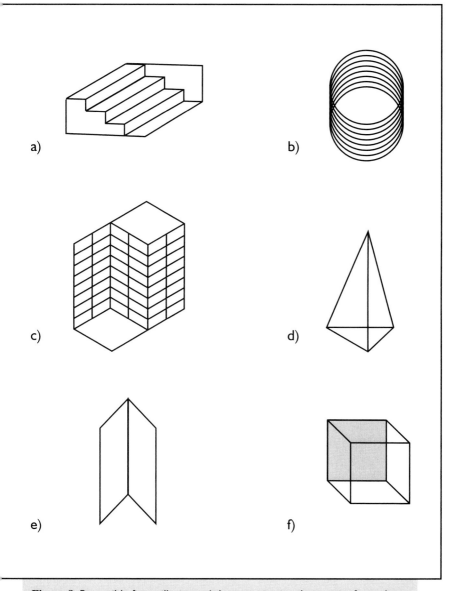

a)

b)

c)

d)

e)

f)

Figure 8. Reversible figure illusions: a) Are you viewing these stairs from above or from below? b) Does the tube open up or down? c) How are these bricks oriented? d) Is this tetrahedron tipped forward or backward? e) On which edges does this folded card rest? f) What is the nature of the illusion you see when you stare at this cube?

a red paper square, about 10 cm (4 in) on a side, on a sheet of white paper. Place a plain sheet of white paper beside the one that has the red square on it. Stand near the two sheets of paper and stare at the red square for 30 seconds. Then shift your gaze to the plain white paper. You will see a cyan (blue-green) square on the paper. The cyan square is called an afterimage. Cyan is the complementary color of red. It contains the other two primary colors of light: green and blue. Having stared at a red square for so long, the cells in your retina that respond to red light are tired. As a result, when you look at a white background, the fatigued cells that react to red light respond less than those that are stimulated by blue and green light. Consequently, you see a cyan square.

What do you think will be the color of the afterimage if you repeat the experiment using a green square? A blue square? A yellow square? A cyan square? A magenta square? A black square? Try it.

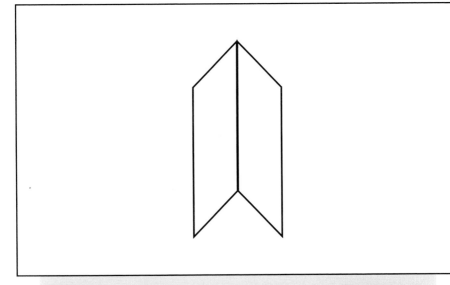

Figure 9. Place a folded index card on a table and look at it with only one eye. You will find that your brain can perceive the card in two different ways.

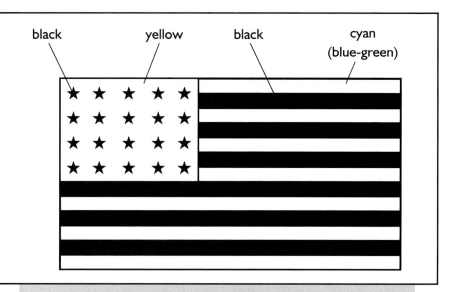

Figure 10. What will the afterimage of this flag look like? The stars are black on a yellow background. The stripes are alternately black and cyan.

Prepare a paper flag using the colors indicated in Figure 10. What colors do you predict will be in the afterimage of this flag?

Afterimages demonstrate that images formed on your retinas persist for a time. Of course, we do not normally stare at an object long enough to "burn" an image onto our retinas. But even in normal light, a retinal image persists for about 0.07 second. Movies are a series of still photographs shown at a rate of 48 views per second. For this reason, actors in movies appear to move normally. The image from one frame remains on the retina long enough to merge with the image in the next frame.

2-6
Vertical-Horizontal and Müller-Lyer Illusions

Figure 11a is sometimes known as the vertical-horizontal illusion, and Figure 11b is known as the Müller-Lyer illusion, for the scientists who devised it. You can use these two illusions to test subjects in a quantitative way.

Using a straight edge, such as a yardstick, make a horizontal line about a foot long on a blackboard or easel. To begin the experiment, record your first subject's name, age, and gender. Then ask your subject to draw a vertical line upward from the center of the horizontal line until the vertical line, according to his estimate, is equal in length to the horizontal line. After the subject has drawn the vertical line, measure it and record his estimate next to his name in your notebook.

Repeat this experiment with as many subjects as possible.

Do all your subjects underestimate the length of the vertical line they believe to be equal in length to the horizontal line? Does your data indicate that older people are better at estimating the vertical length than younger subjects? How about gender? Are girls and women better at making the estimate than boys and men?

The Müller-Lyer illusion can be tested in a quantitative way as well. On each of two thin sheets of white cardboard, draw a straight line with a heavy, dark pen. On one line place large arrow heads at each end. On the other draw an arrow tail at one end. Holding the cardboards on a tabletop as shown in Figure 12, slide one sheet under the other until your subject believes the arrow-tailed line is

Things you will need:

- straight edge, such as a yardstick
- blackboard or easel
- chalk or pen
- ruler
- as many people to serve as subjects as possible
- pen or pencil
- notebook
- 2 thin sheets of white cardboard, each about 12 in x 16 in
- table

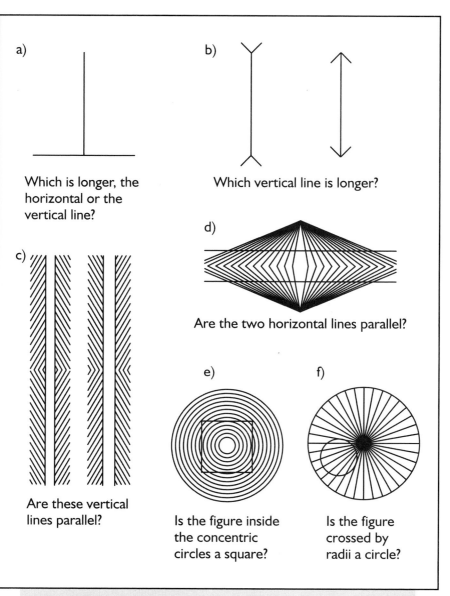

a) Which is longer, the horizontal or the vertical line?

b) Which vertical line is longer?

c) Are these vertical lines parallel?

d) Are the two horizontal lines parallel?

e) Is the figure inside the concentric circles a square?

f) Is the figure crossed by radii a circle?

Figure 11. Which of these drawings are illusions? Can you explain any of them on the basis of the principles about which you have read?

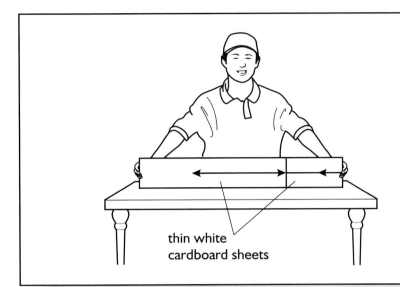

thin white
cardboard sheets

Figure 12. The Müller-Lyer illusion can be tested in a quantitative way using two sheets of cardboard and a tabletop, as shown.

equal in length to the arrow-headed line. Start with the line that has arrow heads much longer than the line with the arrow tail. Move the sheet until the subject tells you the lines are of equal length. Then measure and record your data next to the subject's name.

Do all your subjects underestimate the length of one line they believe to be equal in length to the other line? Does your data indicate that older people are better at estimating equal lengths than younger subjects? How do girls and women compare to boys and men?

2-7*
What Factors Can Affect Perception?

Figure 13 can be perceived as a tetrahedron (a four-sided figure) tipped forward or backward. As you stare at it, you will see its orientation change.

In this experiment you will try to determine whether exercise or caffeine affects the rate at which a subject's perception of the tetrahedron changes. To obtain meaningful results you should test as many people as possible. **Since this experiment involves exercise and the ingestion of caffeine, be sure your subjects are in good physical condition and normally drink caffeinated beverages such as coffee, tea, cola, or cocoa.** Of course, you can only test a subject for one factor during any one experiment. Otherwise you would not know whether the effect, if any, was caused by caffeine or by exercise.

Tell a subject what to expect as he stares at the drawing of the tetrahedron. Be sure he sees both orientations before you begin the experiment.

Once the subject recognizes the two possible ways of perceiving the tetrahedron, ask him to signal you by raising his hand each time his perception of the figure changes. You can use a pencil or pen to make a mark each time the subject signals you over the course of a two-minute period. Dividing the total number of signals by two will give you the rate of perceptual changes in changes per minute.

Things you will need:

- as many people as possible
- Figure 13 (reversible tetrahedron illusion)
- pencil or pen
- notebook
- clock or watch with second hand
- cup
- caffeinated beverage such as coffee, tea, cola, or cocoa

45

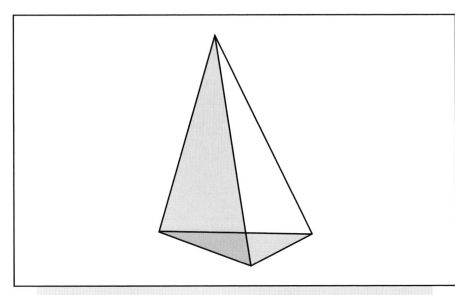

Figure 13. This tetrahedron can be perceived as tipped either forward or back. Use these alternate perceptions to find out how certain factors affect the way we see things.

Next, ask the subject to exercise vigorously by running in place for five minutes. Then repeat the experiment and determine the rate at which his perception of the tetrahedron changes.

To test for the effect of caffeine on perception, measure the rate at which a subject's perception of the figure changes. Then have her drink a full cup of a caffeinated beverage. Wait 15 minutes for the caffeine to be absorbed into the bloodstream before you again measure the rate at which her perception of the figure changes.

Does exercise affect the rate at which a person's perception of the reversible figure changes? Does caffeine?

Exploring on Your Own

Design experiments that will enable you to find out whether the rate of changes in perception is affected by age, gender, or time of day.

3

Emotion

Emotions are the feelings we all have, including happiness, sadness, fear, and anger. An emotion involves changes in the mind and body, and sometimes in the way a person acts. Your brain interprets a situation and you respond both internally and externally. Internally, when you are anxious or nervous, you may experience "butterflies in your stomach," clammy hands, or sweating. You might feel a "lump in your throat" when sad, or you might feel warm when embarrassed. Externally, you may exhibit such muscular activity as clenching your fist, gritting your teeth, or blushing. An emotion is often accompanied by a facial expression such as a smile to indicate happiness, a frown to indicate irritation, or wide eyes that reveal fear.

3-1*
Facial Expressions of Emotion

Do people all over the world feel the same emotions? Do they act the same way when experiencing an emotion, and do they make the same facial expressions when they have these emotions?

Things you will need:

- a large group of subjects
- chalkboard and chalk, or easel and felt-tip pen
- paper and pencils

Our expressions—our smiles, frowns, laughs, gapes, grimaces, snarls, and winks—are intimately tied to our social lives, and these facial expressions have been of special concern to psychologists studying emotion. Charles Darwin (1809–1882), who proposed a theory of evolution nearly 150 years ago, thought that all humans possess a set of facial expressions that come down from the ones our evolutionary ancestors showed in their lives. Many studies have been done to test this theory. Relatively isolated non-Western cultures were investigated. The data indicated that facial expressions might be universal, but the study was not conclusive. The theory may never be fully evaluated because today's communication systems leave very few isolated places in this world.

You probably think of facial expressions as the natural and spontaneous outcome of an underlying emotional state, or perhaps the expression creates the feeling. Of course, we can hide or fake an emotional reaction, but in general when we are happy we smile, and when we are very sad we cry. In part, facial expressions may signify emotions within us; in part, they may be messages we send to others. Perhaps our emotional state primes us to make facial expressions.

Some theorists suggest that facial expressions not only reflect our emotional state but also help produce it. Another view is that facial expressions are primarily a means of communication because they occur when we are in the presence of others or when we think about others.

Gather a group of people. Your classmates might serve as a group if your teacher agrees. Ask for a volunteer to demonstrate facial expressions that reflect different emotions. On a chalkboard or easel write down six emotions (surprise, fear, disgust, anger, happiness, and sadness). Ask the volunteer to display four emotions (listing six will make the chore more difficult for the rest of the class). Emphasize to the volunteer that he or she is to use only facial expressions. There are to be no gestures or body movements. The volunteer silently chooses one emotion from the six and tries to express that emotion through his or her facial expression. The rest of the class writes on a sheet of paper the one emotion from the list of six that they think the volunteer is displaying. You might also ask the class to write the facial characteristics that they think indicates the emotion. This would include the shape or change in eyes, eyebrows, forehead, lips, and so on.

Continue the experiment until the volunteer has demonstrated four emotions. The class should number their responses and the volunteer should write on a sheet of paper, in order, the emotions he or she tried to convey.

How good was the class at guessing the emotions demonstrated? Were some emotions more easily guessed than others?

If possible, try the same experiment with other groups and with different volunteers. Are the results similar? Are some volunteers better than others at showing emotions? Did the class come up with similar descriptions of what the face should look like for different emotions? For example, in the display of surprise, did most people think the lips should form an O? Compare the descriptions and make a list of facial changes for each emotion. Try the experiment again with a different group, but give the volunteer instructions on how to display the emotion based on your list of similarities. Did the instructions improve the volunteer's ability to communicate emotion?

Exploring on Your Own

A fun way to do this experiment, if you have the technology in your school, is to use a computer. Use a digital camera to take pictures of someone displaying the six different emotions mentioned above. Scan the pictures on the computer and add a list of the six possible emotions beside the pictures. Ask your subjects to highlight or record the one they think is being displayed. This approach might enable you to collect much more data. If your school has a computer network and you place your experiment on the network, you could poll the whole school. (Obviously, you would need to get permission to do this.) It would be interesting to see if the grade level of the subjects affected their ability to judge the emotions displayed. You would have to decide if you wanted the same emotions displayed to everyone or if each subject would get a random display of four emotions. Would you use the same faces for all participants to judge or would you have a variety of people model the emotions for the computer?

You could ask the computer participants to write down facial characteristics for the emotions. You could then use a list of their responses to make new photos and redo the experiments. Are the results better? If so, do you think it was because of the list of responses or because the participants just got better at judging emotions? Remember the saying Practice makes perfect.

3-2*
Responses to Emotion

There are two major theories about the cause of our emotions. A common-sense theory suggests that when we are sad, we cry; when we see an uncaged

Things you will need:
* people to serve as subjects
* paper
* pencil

lion, we are scared and our impulse is to scream and run. The emotion causes a behavior such as crying or screaming. According to this theory, our brain's interpretation of an experience causes an emotion, which causes body changes, such as a faster heartbeat, to occur. The second theory turns the first theory upside down. This second theory states that the body change causes the emotion. The subjective feeling of emotion is just the awareness of these body changes. In other words, when we feel our heart beat rapidly, we feel afraid.

Ask some people, such as your classmates, to keep track of any strong emotions they experience over a week. Ask them to be especially careful to record the order of events that led to the emotion and any signs of body changes that accompanied the emotion such as blushing, sweating, trembling, or heart pounding. Ask them if they were aware of their changes (blushing, sweating, trembling, heart pounding) before they felt an emotion, if they felt the emotion first and then became aware of their bodily changes, or if it all happened simultaneously.

Compare the notes recorded by your subjects. Do a majority of them think the emotion came first? Did your findings seem to confirm either of the major theories?

Exploring on Your Own

Experiment 3-2 is subjective because you are dealing with people's feelings and opinions. Can you think of a more objective way to test these two theories of emotion that would not harm participants, physically or emotionally? (You do not want to expose people to highly emotional situations that could be detrimental to their health or upset them.)

4

Personality

Your personality consists of those behaviors, characteristics, and traits by which you are recognized as an individual. It is the basis for your reputation, for the way others see you. The word *personality* comes from the Latin word *persona*, which means "mask." Your personality, based on the Latin, is the mask you present to the world. This implies that a person's outward behavior, which provides the impression he or she makes on others, may not be what the person is really like. In some cases this is true. We all know people who can "put it on." They are able to make a good first impression with teachers or at a social event where they meet important people, but within their family or among close friends, they may exhibit very different behavior.

Behavioral Traits

There are many behavioral traits that make up an individual's personality. Some people are very talkative and outgoing. They are called extroverts. Introverts, on the other hand, are quiet and reserved, even shy. Some people are optimistic about the world around them; others view it with pessimism. People may appear to be happy, sad, or passive. Some are aggressive; some are reserved. These and many other traits make up one's personality. But these traits are not constant. They can change depending on the situation. An extrovert may be quiet at a funeral, and introverts may be more outgoing with close friends. The behavioral traits that constitute a personality reflect a person's average behavior.

Beneath one's behavior are thoughts and feelings, the basis for the actions others observe. People who are empathetic—sensitive, compassionate, and kindhearted—reveal these feelings by their actions. They are supportive, attentive, and willing to listen to others. Their desire to help others is evident from their posture, tone of voice, and expression.

Some people, on the other hand, may fake such behavior in order to be liked or gain the approval of someone they think can help them achieve a goal. Still others may be truly empathetic but think that being helpful means solving problems and giving advice. As a result, they appear insensitive and overbearing to those they most want to help.

The healthiest mental condition belongs to the person whose behavior with others is the same as the feelings he or she has inside. For most of us, however, there are areas of our personality that are viewed differently by others than by ourselves. And there are secret aspects of our personalities that are known only to us and not to the rest of the world. Many believe there are also areas of the personality that remain in the unconscious mind and are known to no one.

Personality and the Unconscious Mind

Many psychiatrists (doctors who treat mental problems) contend that they can bring out thoughts hidden in the unconscious minds of their patients. They use projective tests to try to make contact with unconscious thoughts and desires. In the Rorschach test, for instance, the subject is asked to give his or her reaction to an inkblot. Since the patterns have no meaning, it is assumed that whatever is seen by the subject is the result of his or her unconscious thoughts.

Personality, the Brain, and Chemistry

The brain is the source of all our thoughts and emotions. The personality traits that we exhibit originate in our brains, which are structured according to a pattern found in the genes we inherit. Some psychologists estimate that about half of our personality is the result of our genes. Other parts of our personalities are molded by our environment and culture.

In recent years the chemicals released from brain cells have been identified and their effects on the body determined. The release

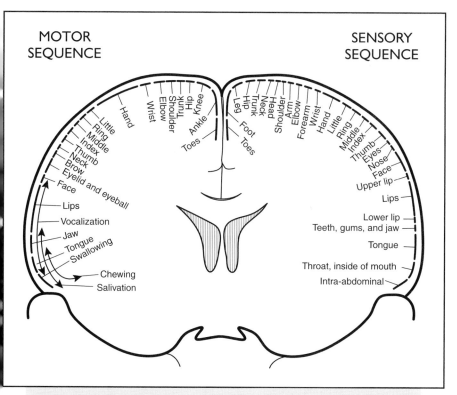

Figure 14. This drawing shows a cross section of the brain through the sensory and motor regions. Specific motor and sensory sequences are indicated. The lengths of the solid bars represent an estimate of the relative areas of the cortex that serve each part of the body.

of the chemical dopamine into the brain is associated with the outgoing, pleasure-seeking behavior characteristic of extroverts. Low levels of dopamine have the opposite effect. An enzyme, monoamine oxidase, counteracts dopamine, and high levels of this substance are characteristic of sedate personalities. Nerve impulses arising in the frontal lobe of the brain (see Figure 14) can inhibit the production of a substance called serotonin and cause impulsive behavior such as irritability, aggression, and violence.

The male sex hormone testosterone is believed to be the reason that aggressive behavior is more common in men than in women. It is mostly young men who engage in such contact sports as football, rugby, and hockey. It is also males who commit 90 percent of all violent crimes.

Among early humans, aggressive behavior from high levels of testosterone helped people survive. The males could hunt for food and drive off animal and human predators. Such aggressive behavior is far less important in today's world, where food is available in stores and national armies provide protection.

4-1*
Extrovert or Introvert?

Psychologists often give tests in an effort to determine an individual's personality. For example, questions can be designed to determine if a person is an extrovert or an introvert. Most people are somewhere in between. They are sometimes outgoing, sometimes shy or reserved, sometimes indifferent. A test to determine if a person is an extrovert or an introvert could be made from items such as those listed in Table 2.

Things you will need:
- Table 2
- pen or pencil
- paper
- people to serve as subjects

How would you expect an extrovert to respond to each of these items? How would you expect an introvert to respond?

Add more items and questions of your own design in order to develop a test that will determine whether someone is an extrovert, introvert, or neither.

To find out if your test is useful in identifying extroverts and introverts, try it with people you know well.

If your test seems useful in identifying extroverts and introverts, try it on a number of people you do not know well. If it does not, try to change those items that are not useful and add new items that are effective in identifying these personality traits.

Exploring on Your Own
Design and carry out a test to determine the strength of a person's self-esteem.

Table 2: An example questionnaire to determine whether a person is an extrovert or introvert.

I. A number of paired statements are listed below. Circle the statement, a or b, that you feel best represents you.

1. a) I sometimes like to be alone.
   b) I do not like to be alone.
2. a) I prefer to have a few close friends.
   b) I prefer to have many casual friends.
3. a) I don't like it when people dare me to do something.
   b) I enjoy it when people dare me to do something.
4. a) I hate to sell things.
   b) I enjoy selling things.
5. a) If I were to be involved in a play, I'd prefer to build or design the props.
   b) If I were to be involved in a play, I'd want to be one of the actors on stage.

II. A number of statements are listed below. Answer each one by writing the response—A B, C, or D—that best fits you.

A. Strongly disagree	C. Agree to some extent
B. Disagree to some extent	D. Strongly agree

1. I see myself as talkative.
2. I see myself as reserved.
3. I see myself as enthusiastic about most things I do.
4. I see myself as sociable and outgoing.
5. I tend to reflect on most things before talking about them.

4-2
Optimist or Pessimist?

You can also design a test to find out whether a person is an optimist or a pessimist. For example, pictures with captions such as those in Figure 15 can be used in

Things you will need:

• pen or pencil

• paper

• word processor

such a test. Additional items could be made from items such as those found in Table 3. An optimist can be expected to respond with a as a choice; a pessimist would choose a b response.

For each type of test, add more questions of your own design. Then try to think of different types of questions that will also reveal if a person is optimistic or pessimistic. When you have enough questions to make a test that will take a subject about ten minutes to finish, try the test on a number of different subjects. To find out if your test is useful in identifying optimists and pessimists, you will first have to try it with people you know well.

If your test seems useful in identifying optimists and pessimists, try it on a number of people you do not know well. If the test does not seem accurate, develop new test questions.

Examine each of the pictures below. Quickly decide whether it is (a) or (b) that best describes your response to the picture.

The soda bottle is
a) half full.
b) half empty.

The tree is falling
a) beside the house.
b) on the house.

a) Holidays ahead
b) Slippery road ahead

a) A new idea
b) A higher electric bill

Figure 15. The beginnings of a test to determine whether someone is an optimist or a pessimist.

Table 3: Samples of two types of questions to evaluate a person for optimism or pessimism are shown below. You can probably think of other types of questions to test for this personality trait.

I. A number of statements are listed below. Each statement is followed by two responses. Circle the response, a or b, that you would choose.

   1. The score is 12–6, it's the last inning, and your home team is behind. You think:
      a) We should hope for a big ninth-inning rally.
      b) We should leave the game to beat the traffic.

   2. When you see the word *row*, you think of
      a) items arranged horizontally on a line.
      b) an argument.

   3. The word *trick* brings to mind
      a) magic.
      b) deception.

   4. You are on vacation. You wake up and it's raining. You think:
      a) A great day to read, play cards, or play board games.
      b) I might as well sleep, there's nothing to do.

II. Answer the following as true or false by circling T or F after each statement.

   1. In times of uncertainty, I usually expect everything will turn out all right.   T   F
   2. If something can go wrong for me, you can be sure it will.   T   F
   3. I think my future is a bright one.   T   F
   4. I seldom expect things to go my way.   T   F

4-3
Revealing Inkblots

You read earlier that psychologists use the Rorschach test to try to reach a person's unconscious mind. The results of such a projective test can be properly interpreted only by someone trained in clinical

Things you will need:

- Figure 16
- paper
- pen
- ink
- as many people as possible

psychology or psychiatry. You can do some reading in an encyclopedia or textbook or on the Internet about how subjects' responses reveal their mental state. You may find it interesting to ask people to look at inkblots, such as the one in Figure 16, and ask them what they see.

What do you see when you look at Figure 16? Ask as many people as possible, one at a time, to tell you what they see when they

Figure 16. What do you see when you look at this inkblot?

look at the figure. What do they say? Do any two or more people interpret the inkblot in the same way?

Make some inkblots of your own and ask people to tell you what they see. You can either design the shape of the inkblots or simply let ink fall on a piece of paper in a random way.

5

Learning and Memory

Psychologists define *learning* as a relatively permanent change in behavior or knowledge resulting from experience. There are three basic types of learning: classical conditioning, operant conditioning, and cognitive learning. In classical conditioning a person learns by his response to an outside experience, a stimulus. In operant conditioning one learns from the results of behavior. In cognitive learning a person gets information by reasoning and thinking.

Memory involves the encoding, storage, and retrieval of information and past experiences. Encoding involves organizing the information we take in. Storage is the process of retaining that information. Retrieval is the ability to recognize or recall what has been stored. We use memory to record events in our lives as well as the information and skills related to those experiences.

Classical Conditioning

Ivan Pavlov's research with dogs was the first scientific investigation of conditioning. Pavlov, working at the beginning of the twentieth century, placed meat powder on a dog's tongue to stimulate a reflex flow of saliva. If he rang a bell just before placing the meat powder on the tongue, the dog would soon begin to salivate at the sound of the bell even without the meat powder stimulus. Pavlov called the meat powder the unconditioned stimulus (UCS). It caused the unconditioned response (UCR)—saliva flow. At the beginning of this experiment, the neutral stimulus (NS), the bell, did not produce any response (NR). During conditioning, the bell was repeatedly presented just before the meat powder, the unconditioned stimulus, was placed on the dog's tongue. After conditioning, the bell became a conditioned stimulus (CS) that caused salivation as a conditioned response (CR) even if the unconditioned stimulus (meat powder) was not given. The equations below summarize the conditioning process.

$$\text{UCS} \nrightarrow \text{UCR}$$
(meat powder)   (saliva flow)

$$\text{NS} \nrightarrow \text{NR}$$
(bell)   (no response)

$$\text{NS} + \text{UCS} \nrightarrow \text{UCR}$$
(bell)   (meat powder)   (saliva flow)

The neutral stimulus (bell) soon becomes a conditioned stimulus, so that

$$\text{CS} \nrightarrow \text{CR}$$
(bell)   (saliva flow)

5-1
Conditioning

In classical conditioning a stimulus can produce a response that it would not normally cause. You can do an experiment in classical conditioning using the same knee response that a doctor uses to test reflexes. Carry out several trials with a subject. Ask your subject to sit on a chair or table high enough so that her feet are off the floor. Lightly tap her knee with the rubber hammer. Just before you tap her knee, a friend serving as

Things you will need:

- several people to serve as subjects
- a friend
- rubber hammer or suitable substitute such as a stick inserted into a large one-hole rubber stopper
- paper
- pencil
- something to serve as a conditioned stimulus such as a word, a pencil that can be tapped, or a bell

your assistant can ring a bell or strike a table with a pencil. After a number of trials, the sound should produce the response without your having to strike the subject's leg with the rubber hammer. The subject is now reacting to a conditioned stimulus she hears, not to the unconditioned stimulus she feels.

How many trials do you think it will take before the sound becomes a conditioned stimulus? Try it out and see if your prediction is correct.

How might you eliminate the conditioned reflex? How many trials are needed before the conditioned stimulus no longer produces the conditioned response?

Operant Conditioning

B. F. Skinner (1904–1990) developed the term *operant conditioning* in the 1930s. Operant conditioning is a form of learning in which a behavior becomes more or less probable depending on its consequences. The behavior elicited depends on the consequences that follow. There are different types of consequences, but we will focus on positive reinforcement, which is the easiest to observe and the most ethical.

In positive reinforcement, there is an increase in the probability of a behavior that is followed by a desirable consequence. You probably know a teacher who gives stickers for good work or behavior. That would be an example of positive reinforcement. Another example is your parents' permission to let you watch television after you finish your homework. You are more likely to complete your homework if you know that a desirable activity will follow.

Animal trainers use positive reinforcement to train animals. For example, dogs do not normally jump through hoops. Trainers use a process called shaping to elicit the desired behavior. Shaping involves rewarding the subject for doing something related to the objective. Eventually reinforcement follows performance of the desired conduct.

To train a dog to jump through a hoop, the trainer first rewards the dog for coming close to the hoop, then for stepping in the hoop, then for walking through the hoop, and finally for jumping through the hoop. Obviously, the desired behavior has to be one that the subject can perform. You could not train your dog to use a knife and fork to eat its food, but you could train it to shake hands or roll over. Make sure that you are consistent with your reinforcement and that it is working to condition your subject. Praise and small bits of food are positive reinforcers to a dog or other pet.

It will take many trials to train an animal to do a trick. And you must remember to take into consideration the animal's age. The old saying You can't teach an old dog a new trick is not necessarily true. However, if your dog is old or arthritic, do not try to teach it to do a trick that could be physically painful to perform. Also, a very young puppy may not be developmentally ready to learn the skill you want to establish. Furthermore, you must take into consideration the kind of animal you want to train. Some animals, such as dogs, are easier to train than others, such as rabbits.

Cognitive Learning and Memory

Classical and operant conditioning are concerned with changing behavior. Cognitive learning is more closely associated with the acquisition of knowledge or information. This type of learning requires memory because acquired information is stored for retrieval in our brains. We use our memory to record our experiences and to gain information and skills from experience. Through our memory we can bring to mind an event or information from the past.

5-2
Memory and Meaning

Psychologists say that remembering a list of words is easier when those words go together in a meaningful way. In this experiment you can test that idea by using the two word lists provided in Table 4.

Divide a number of people who are all about the same age into two groups. The groups

should be separated so that one group cannot hear the other. Read list A to one group and then give them one minute to write down as many words as they can remember from the list. Make sure you read the list in an evenly spaced manner.

Meanwhile, have a friend read list B to the second group and give them one minute to write down all the words they can remember from their list. Compare the abilities of the two groups to remember the middle words. The group that had list B will probably remember more of the words from the middle of the list than will the group that had list A. Can you explain why?

Compare the total number of words each group was able to remember. Find the average number of words remembered by each group. Is there a significant difference? Can you explain any difference?

Were people more likely to remember the first few words of a list even though they did not have any particular meaning? Psychologists call this the primacy effect. Were people more likely to remember the last words of the lists? This is called the recency effect.

Table 4: Two word lists, A and B.

Word List A	Word List B
Funny	Funny
Good	Good
Little	Little
Polite	Polite
Red	Bacon
Sweet	Lettuce
Old	Tomato
Honest	Honest
Weak	Weak
Strange	Strange
Interesting	Interesting
Slow	Slow
Weathered	Weathered
Large	Large
Unhappy	Unhappy

5-3*
Maze Learning

You have probably heard of psychologists' experimenting with a mouse running through a maze. The mouse tries to reach a reward by learning to run the maze through a series of trial-and-error explorations. People perform the same sort of trial-and-error explorations when learning new motor or verbal skills, such as riding a bicycle or reciting a poem. In this experiment you will find out how quickly people can learn to move successfully through a maze like the one shown in Figure 17.

Things you will need:

- several people to serve as subjects
- blindfold
- maze
- table
- chair
- stylus (swizzle stick or unsharpened pencil)
- stopwatch, or watch with a second hand
- lined paper
- pencil

You will need to test subjects individually. Of course, the subjects should not see the maze before the experiment. Blindfold the subject and seat him at a table in front of the maze. Put the stylus in his hand and place the stylus at the beginning of the maze, which he should note is a circle by moving the stylus. Inform him that the goal is a circular space similar to the starting position. Tell the subject he is being timed and there are paths that are dead ends. His goal is to maneuver through the maze as quickly as possible using only the hand that holds the stylus. Let the subject repeat his trip through the maze until he has made three trips without going into a dead end or turning the wrong way. Time each trip and keep track of the number of errors. Do not ask a subject to do more than 20 trials.

Graph the results of the trials for each individual on a line graph. Have one graph show the time taken to complete the maze versus

71

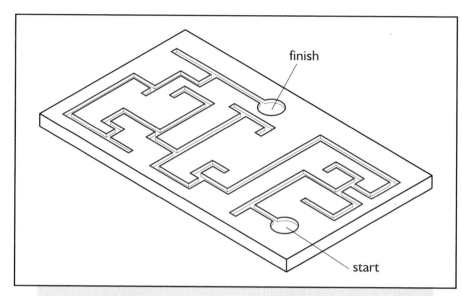

finish

start

Figure 17. A maze like the one shown in this drawing can be made from a board into which a grooved path is burned or cut. (A shop student or teacher may be able to help you make the maze.) A swizzle stick or an unsharpened pencil can serve as a stylus for "running" the maze.

the number of previous trials. Another graph can show the number of errors versus the number of previous trials.

Does the time taken per trial and the number of errors decrease as the trials progress? Did subjects show steady improvement or were there trials where no improvement took place?

Exploring on Your Own

Design an experiment to find out whether the speed of learning to "run" the maze is related to the age of the participant.

Design experiments to test other factors that might affect the rate at which people learn to move through the maze. For example, does gender affect the rate?

5-4*
Backward Alphabet

Learning new material for school or learning a new skill takes practice. You have to practice writing the words in a new spelling list; you have to practice to successfully do a flip in gymnastics. The old saying Practice makes perfect is true. But are there

Things you will need:
- several people to serve as subjects
- lined sheets of paper numbered 1–10 for each subject
- pencils
- stopwatch, or watch with a second hand

ways to practice that are better than others? Should you take a break and let the information soak in, or should you practice nonstop for an extended period? This experiment will help you answer such questions.

Ask a number of subjects to write the alphabet backward, from Z to A. Give them one minute to complete the task. Immediately after the minute has passed, ask them to do it again. Continue until they have completed ten trials.

Next, have a second group start the same way by writing the alphabet backward. After one minute, let them rest for a minute. Then ask them to write the alphabet backward again. Continue this sequence of writing and resting for ten trials. How do the results of the two groups compare?

How can you represent the results on a graph? Which group was more successful in completing the task? Did both groups continue to get better as the trials progressed?

Based on the results of your experiment, should you take a break and let the information soak in when learning a task or should you practice nonstop for an extended period?

Exploring on Your Own

Design an experiment to find out if fatigue is a factor in learning to write the alphabet backward.

Design an experiment to find out whether taking breaks or practicing nonstop is the better way to learn a physical activity.

5-5
Interference or Reinforcement in Learning

Sometimes what a person has learned makes it difficult to learn something new. This is known as interference to learning. Sometimes what a person has learned makes it easier to learn a new task. This is known as learning reinforcement. This experiment will allow you to explore the effects of previous learning on new learning. Pair up a large number of people. Give each pair a sheet of paper, a pencil or pen, and a stopwatch. (If the room where you are experimenting has a large clock with a second hand, that timepiece can serve for all the pairs.) One person in the pair will be the subject and one will be the tester. The subject's task is to print the alphabet in capital letters backward (starting with Z and ending with A) and upside down (so that when the paper is inverted the letters will appear to be correctly written; see Figure 18). The tester will take the sheet as she finishes and fold the paper down after each trial so that the subject cannot just copy what he did on the last trial.

Things you will need:

- pencils or pens
- paper
- several stopwatches, or watches or clocks with a second hand, or a clock with a second hand visible to all in a large room
- large number of people

The subject does the task ten times. The first and tenth time he is to do it with the hand with which he does not usually write. For trials 2 to 9, he is to use the hand he prefers to use for writing.

If possible, pair off a classroom of students so that you will have a lot of data quickly. Have each pair do ten trials. After each trial, the tester should record the time in seconds that it took the subject to complete the task and the number of letters that were written correctly. The subject should have a short rest period of about half a minute between trials while the tester scores the results. Each error should be subtracted from 26 to obtain a score. Tally up the scores

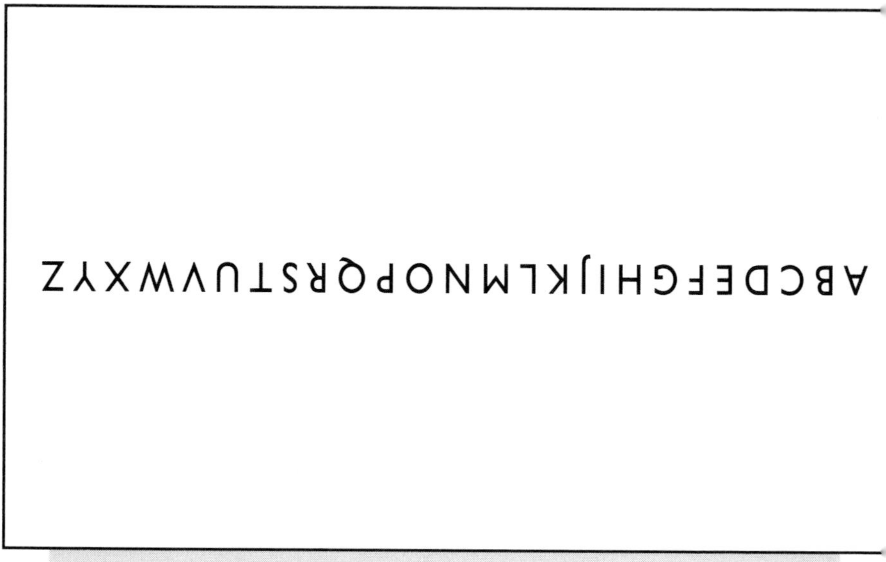

A B C D E F G H I J K L M N O P Q R S T U V W X Y Z

Figure 18. The alphabet written upside down and backward in capital letters. Turn it over and it will appear to be correctly written.

for each trial. Compare the scores and times for the first and last trial. Is there any difference? Did writing with the preferred hand help (reinforce) the performance of the other hand? Or did writing with the preferred hand hinder (interfere with) learning to write the upside down and backward alphabet with the other hand?

Did some people do a lot better on this task than others? What might be a reason for that? Did it make a difference if the person was right-handed or left-handed?

Did the subjects get better in the middle trials with their preferred hand?

Do you have any evidence that there was a transfer of skill from one hand to the other? If you do, what is that evidence?

5-6*
Belongingness in Learning

Psychologists claim that learning is faster if the items learned are perceived as belonging together. Words in a sentence are understood to belong together after they are heard. To test this

Things you will need:
• several people
• paper
• pencil

theory of belongingness, try the following experiment. In the experiment the association between two words in the same sentence will be compared to the association between two words that are in different sentences.

Read the following sentences, or similar ones, to a group of subjects. Try to read the sentences at a steady pace so that there is no difference in the time period between sentences.

Johnny rides a bicycle.

Sally rides a horse.

Robert rides a spaceship.

Adam rides a train.

Barbara rides a car.

William rides a subway.

Now ask the following questions. Answers are in parentheses.

1. Which word followed *Sally rides a*? (horse)

2. Which word followed *rides a car*? (William)

3. Which word followed *Robert rides a*? (spaceship)

4. Which word followed *rides a train*? (Barbara)

The number of correct answers to *#2* and *#4* test the association between words in different sentences.

Were there more correct answers to #1 and #3, as the theory of belongingness would predict?

Exploring on Your Own

Is there any difference in results if you read more sentences to the group? Is there any difference in results if you read fewer sentences?

5-7*
Active or Short-term Memory with Numbers

Active or short-term memory is the ability to remember something for a short time. You might guess that our ability to remember items, especially unrelated or meaningless details, is limited. In this experiment you will have an opportunity to test this assumption.

Things you will need:
- several people
- pencils or pens
- paper

Gather a group of people and pass out paper and pencils to them. You will read a list of unrelated numbers to the group. Start with 4 digits and increase by one up to 12 digits. After you read the first group of 4 digits, immediately ask the group to write the digits you have read. They should not start to write until you have finished reading the group of digits. Repeat with the next group of 5 digits and continue with all the groups in the same manner. You can use the following list of digits or you can prepare your own list.

6 2 9 5

3 5 8 4 2

7 2 6 8 1 3

5 9 6 3 5 2 4

2 6 9 1 4 7 3 8

1 7 4 2 8 6 3 5 9

8 5 2 4 1 9 6 7 3 5

4 3 8 2 7 1 4 9 6 2 5

9 4 1 7 9 5 6 8 1 3 4 2

When checking the subjects' lists, all the numbers in a line must be in the correct order or that line is considered wrong. How many numbers can the average person immediately recall? It will probably be six or seven if your results are similar to other investigators'.

Were some participants better at remembering long lines of numbers than others? If there were such people, ask them if they know why they were able to remember the numbers.

Exploring on Your Own

Design and carry out an experiment to find out if the rate at which you read the numbers affects a person's ability to remember them.

5-8
Chunking in Memory

Chunking (putting bits of information together in a meaningful way) may help people overcome their limited short-term memory. This experiment will help you find out if it does.

Things you will need:
- several people
- pencils or pens
- paper

Pass out paper and pencils to a group of people. Read the list of letters below to the group. Be sure to read the letters at a steady, even pace. Immediately after you finish reading the letters, but not before, ask them to write those letters in the same order in which they were read.

TCNNPHDSATNBCT

What was the average number of letters the subjects were able to remember?

Now read the subjects the same list of letters organized as follows. Be sure to pause briefly between each of the six groups.

T CNN PHD SAT NBC T

Again, ask the group to write the letters in the same order they were read.

Compare the results after the first reading with the results after the second reading. How do they compare?

In the second trial, you read the letters as six chunks of information instead of 14 individual letters. The Ts were at each end, and then there were four groups of three letters that had meaning. (CNN and NBC are television stations, PhD is a doctorate degree, and SAT is a scholastic test you have probably heard of!)

After you have made the participants aware of chunking, read to them the similar list shown below at a steady, even pace. Do you think they will remember more letters now that they are aware of chunking?

ZBLTPBSNFLCBSZ

Compare the correct letters remembered on this trial with the first trial. Did everyone get some of the chunks? Did anyone get all the chunks shown below?

Z BLT PBS NFL CBS Z

Is it easier to find meaning in letters than in numbers? What evidence do you have? If you assigned letters to numbers, would it be easier to remember strings of numbers?

5-9*
Phone Number Mnemonics

Do you have trouble remembering phone numbers? Many people do. Mnemonics may help. Mnemonics are techniques that help people remember things. They include various forms of organization, visual

Things you will need:
- several people
- 18 index cards
- watch with a second hand
- pencils or pens
- paper

imagery, and using rhyme and rhythm. This experiment has to do with remembering phone numbers.

Phone numbers used to begin with a word. The first two letters of the word were the letters on the same space on the phone as the numbers. For instance, MAple represented 62. People found it easier to remember a word and five numbers than seven numbers. You will compare your subjects' ability to remember all-digit phone numbers, those prefixed with two letters in place of digits, and ones with the number converted into a mnemonic code of letters.

On one group of six index cards, write all-digit phone numbers, such as those in Table 5. Write one phone number on each card. On a second group of cards, write the same six phone numbers but change the first two numbers into the letters found with those numbers on the phone pad. You cannot use phone numbers that have a 1 or a 0, since there are no letters for those numbers on the pad. On the last set of index cards, write these phone numbers again but convert the numbers into letters that match the numbers on the phone pad.

You will need three groups of subjects. One group will be given the all-digit cards, one group will use the cards with the word and numbers, and one group will use the all-letter cards. You will need to test the participants individually, so you may want to have a couple of friends help you do the test. Make sure everyone uses the same procedures.

Table 5. Three ways to express phone numbers.

Prefixed by Letters	All Digits	Mnemonic Code
MAple 3-4729	623-4729	MAD I PAW
CIrcle 8-6386	248-6386	CIT OF TO
LAngdon 6-3463	526-3463	LAND HOE
CHapter 4-2924	244-2924	CHI A WAH
DRagon 6-7648	376-7648	DROP NIT
AUtumn 8-6763	288-6763	AUTO ROD

Show each card in a group to the subject for five seconds. After you have shown all six cards, give the subject one minute to write down as many of the phone numbers he or she can recall. Do this procedure five times, varying the order of the index cards from trial to trial.

Compare the three groups. To count as correct, all the numbers or letters of the phone number must be written in the proper order. What, if anything, can you conclude from the data?

What do you think you will find if you asked the three groups to write down as many of the six phone numbers as they can recall after 24 hours?

Exploring on Your Own

Why are local phone numbers limited to seven digits?

Why did phone companies stop using introductory words as part of phone numbers?

5-10*
Exposure and Encoding

Being exposed to an experience or information does not necessarily lead to its storage and retrieval in your memory. It needs to be organized. Encoding is the organization of experience and information to help people remember.

Things you will need:

- several people
- pencils or pens
- paper
- a coin for each participant
- Figure 19
- copier

Most people remember very little about the appearance of items they are exposed to many, many times. Take any United States coin, such as a penny, and ask a subject some questions about one of its sides. The following questions pertain to the heads side of a penny, but you can use any common coin you want—a quarter, dime, or nickel.

Most people are aware that on a penny there is a profile of Abraham Lincoln, so you can give subjects this information. Then ask them to write answers to the following questions.

1. Which way does Lincoln face on the penny, left or right?

2. Is there anything written below his profile? If so, what?

3. Is there anything written above his profile? If so, what?

4. Is there anything written to the left of his face? If so, what?

5. Is there anything written to the right of his face? If so, what?

Most people will struggle with the answers. When they are finished, give each subject a penny so that they can check their answers.

Do you think people would do better if they were able to see different pictures of a penny (see Figure 19) and guess which one was correct? Make copies of Figure 19 for your subjects. Then ask new subjects to choose the penny they think is the correct

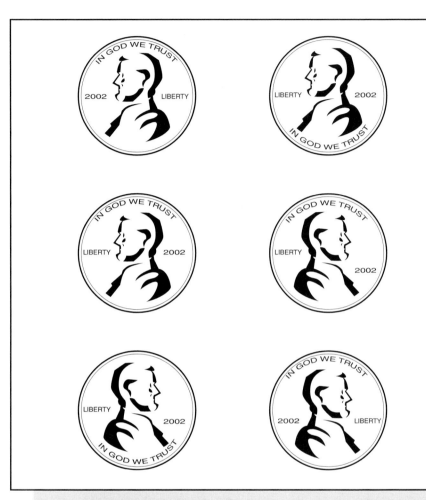

Figure 19. Which drawing represents the real Lincoln penny?

drawing of a real penny. Compare the answers of these subjects to the those who had to answer questions without pictures. Does a visual image seem to help?

Exploring on Your Own

Is one coin better remembered than other coins? Design and conduct an experiment to find out.

6

Thought and Thinking

Psychologists define *thinking* as the ability to reason or reflect. We think every time we solve a problem, judge the truth of a statement, or consider the pros and cons of a situation before making a decision. To perform any of these actions we draw on what we already know. If a situation is one we have encountered before, we can employ the thought processes we used before. If the position we are in is unfamiliar but resembles others we have encountered, we can draw on more general knowledge. However, we are not always as rational and logical as we might think. Past experience and learning can influence and interfere with our thinking, as we will see.

6-1*
The Stroop Effect

Once we learn to read, we automatically read any words we see. Sometimes reading gets in the way of our thinking process because we cannot help reading even when we don't want to. The Stroop effect shows this problem with our thinking and how it can affect the speed at which we process information.

Things you will need:
- pens with different colored ink
- paper
- stopwatch, or watch with second hand
- several people to serve as subjects

Print some nonsense letter groups in colored ink on paper. Some examples are given below. A suggested color for each letter group is given in parentheses. Have four columns of words 12 lines long. (We have provided possible sample letter groups for the first two lines. You will have to make up the next ten lines.) Also prepare a list of the colors of letter groups that you can use for checking. Use a watch to determine how long it takes for the person to tell you the correct color of all the letter groups in the list.

PLG (green)   WKN (blue)   WVD (brown)   BLG (red)

TPY (brown)   ZMG (red)   LHBF (green)   QOX (blue)

This part of the experiment should move along quickly. What is the average time for a subject to state the colors of all the letter groups?

Now do the same thing using real words. Again, examples for the first two lines are provided. You will need to write the next ten.

SPOON (red)   OAK (green)   PONY(blue)   CHILD (brown)

TABLE (green)   BABY (brown)   TOY (red)   BELL (blue)

How long does it take for the average subject to correctly name, for all the words, the color of the ink in which each word is printed?

Now prepare lists of words that are the names of colors. However, print them in a different color than the word. Repeat the directions again at this point so that a subject clearly knows that he is to name the color of the ink used to print the word, not the word itself. Again, the first two lines are provided. You will have to write the next ten.

GREEN (red)   BLUE (brown)   BROWN (green)   RED (brown)

BROWN (green)   RED (blue)   GREEN (red)   BLUE (brown)

This part of the experiment will take longer than the other two parts because of the Stroop effect. Our brains naturally want to read the words and it will take some time before the thinking process will enable the subject to focus on the color of the ink rather than the word.

What was the average time for a subject to name the colors of the words in each of the first two trials? What was the average time for subjects to name the colors of the words in the last trial, where the words were the names of colors? How did the Stroop effect affect the speed at which the colors could be named?

Exploring on Your Own

Design and conduct an experiment to find out if the Stroop effect occurs with clusters of numbers in place of words. Suppose you had clusters of numbers in place of letters arranged in the same way as in Experiment 6-1. The subject should tell you how many numbers are in each cluster. For example, if the cluster is 777, the subject should say, "Three," not "Seven, seven, seven."

You might also test for the Stroop effect when symbols are used in place of letters or numbers. Some examples are given below with the answers in parentheses.

(4) $$$ (3)   % % (2)   &&&&& (5)

Is the Stroop effect as powerful using symbols and numbers as it was using the names of colors?

6-2
The Matchstick Problem

Different types of problems call upon different skills. And different people bring different points of view and past problem-solving experiences to new problems. People carry beliefs and habits with them whenever they approach a problem. We can be misled by our assumptions. In this experiment we will test whether the way material is presented can make a difference in the ability to solve a problem.

Things you will need:

* several people to serve as subjects
* 6 wooden matchsticks for each participant
* table
* small glasses or cups to hold the matchsticks upright
* pencils or pens
* paper

You will need to test subjects individually. For half the people you test, place six matchsticks on a table in a straight row in front of them, as shown in Figure 20a. For the other half, the six matchsticks should be standing upright in a small glass or cup on the table, as shown in Figure 20b. The challenge is the same for both arrangements. Each subject is to arrange the six matchsticks so that they make four equilateral triangles, with each side of the triangle equal to the length of one matchstick. (The solution is shown in Figure 20c.) Time the individual subjects and then find the average time to solve for each arrangement of matches. If a subject does not find the solution within 15 minutes, go ahead and give them the solution.

Did the subjects that were presented with the matchsticks in a row have more difficulty finding the three-dimensional answer? Did there appear to be a "mental set" of keeping the matchsticks in two dimensions for those subjects? Did presenting the materials in three dimensions seem to help the subjects find the solution, or were there no differences in the two groups' abilities to solve the problem?

If the experiments were conducted in groups of three or four individuals, do you think that would improve the ability to find

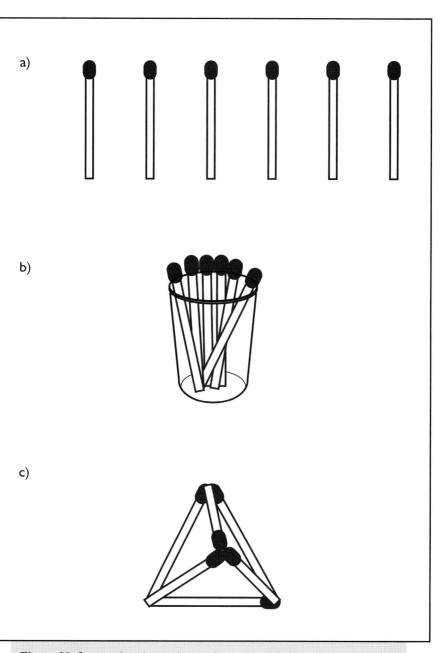

Figure 20. Six matchsticks can be used to pose a problem that will require some thought.

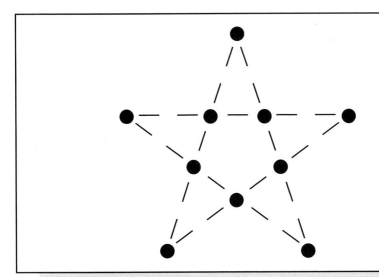

Figure 21. The solution to the apple tree problem is shown here.

the solution? If you think so, would it be as effective for each presentation of the matchsticks? Try it! Were you right?

Would subjects arrive at the solution more quickly if you had them do a warm-up activity? To find out, have two more groups work on the following sample warm-up problem before they are exposed to the matchstick problem.

Sample Warm-up Problem

A farmer wants to plant ten apple trees on a flat section of land. They have to be planted in a pattern so that the ten trees form five straight rows, with four trees in each row. (Hint: Some trees will be in more than one row of trees.)

The solution is shown in Figure 21.

Finally, try giving this problem *after* the matchstick problem. Does one problem seem to work better as a warm-up problem for the other problem?

Having observed both groups, did you see any "mental set" or assumption that had to be broken before the solution could be found?

Development of the Thinking Process

Our thinking processes develop over time. We start at a very concrete level, but as we get older we are able to think more about ideas. Try this experiment on two children of different ages to see how they respond. It is important that you record but not try to influence their answers to the questions you pose.

Administer the same three tests to each child. Do the tests separately so that one child is not influenced by the other.

Start with 20 identical pennies or poker chips. Place a row of ten of them in front of the child. Ask him to make an identical row (see Figure 22a). Ask the child if the two rows have the same number or if one row has more. Do not move on until the child agrees that the two rows have equal numbers.

Things you will need:

- 1 child between the ages of 3 and 5 and 1 child between the ages of 8 and 10
- 20 identical items such as pennies or poker chips
- 2 identical clear drinking cups, and 1 clear drinking cup that is taller and narrower than the other 2, but will hold the same volume
- 3 cups of a colored liquid such as juice
- large ball of clay
- paper
- pencil or pen

Now rearrange the items as shown in Figure 22b. Ask the child if the rows have the same number or if one row has more than the other. If the child says one row has more, ask which row has more and where it came from. If the child thinks the rows have the same number, ask the child to explain why. Make sure to record all the child's answers.

Next, conduct another test. Pour equal amounts of liquid into two identical cups. Ask the child if each cup has the same amount. If she does not think they do, adjust the volume until the child says both cups have the same amount of liquid. Then pour the liquid from one cup into the taller, narrower cup. Put that cup next to the other

Figure 22. Rearrange the pennies from what is shown in (a) to what is shown in (b).

one that has liquid in it. Again ask the child if the two cups have the same amount of liquid or if one has more. If the child says one has more, ask which one. Ask the child why he or she thinks the cups have the same amount of liquid or different amounts. Be sure to record the child's responses.

Take a ball of clay and divide it into two equal amounts. Make sure the child agrees that the two amounts are the same. (Rolling the clay into balls can help the child decide when the amounts are equal.) Give one half of the clay to the child and ask him to roll it into a hot dog. After the child has done this, ask him if the two amounts of clay are the same or if one has more. If the child says one piece of clay has more than the other, ask which one has more. Then ask the child to explain why the amounts are the same or different. Record the child's answers.

How did the younger child's answers compare with those of the older child? What thinking skill does this experiment show develops with maturation?

6-4*
Dreams

Dreams are trains of thought or images that occur during sleep. There are two types of sleep, deep sleep and light sleep. They are

characterized by different brain waves. If you are awakened during deep sleep, you probably will not remember any dreams. If you are awakened during light sleep, you will nearly always remember a dream. Light sleep is also called REM sleep for the rapid eye movement that scientists have found occurs then. REM sleep happens in most species of mammals that have been studied. Does this mean that these animals dream? No one knows for certain, but many people who own dogs think their pets dream because the dogs whimper and have muscle movements in their legs that make it appear that they are dreaming.

In ancient times dreams were thought to foretell the future. More recently, in the early twentieth century, Sigmund Freud (1856–1939) thought dreams were expressions of secret desires. Dreams are hard to understand because they are made up of symbols. Freud attempted to explain the hidden meanings of dreams by interpreting the symbols. Carl Jung (1875–1961), a contemporary of Freud, did not believe that dreams conceal secret desires. He felt that dreams were just a form of human expression, similar to poetry.

Some who study sleep think dreams are a way of processing information. We are exposed to so many stimuli while awake that our brains cannot process them all. Dreams may be a way of examining and sorting through all the impressions and experiences of the day and storing the important ones.

What do you think dreams are? Keep a record of the hours of sleep you get each night and your dreams over the course of a month. The best way to remember dreams is to keep paper and pencil by your bed so that you can write down the dreams you remember when you awaken. If you wake up during the night and remember a dream, try to write it down. That way you will not forget it by the time you wake up in the morning. Are the dreams you remember related to your day's activities? Are they related to the amount of sleep you get?

Exploring on Your Own

Experiment 6-4 suggests that dreams can be easily forgotten. To see if that is true, divide a number of people into two groups. Have one group write down their dreams immediately after they wake up in the morning or during the night. Tell the other group to write down their dreams in the morning after they have written down the date, current weather, and their schedule for the day. Ask the groups to do this for one week. After a week, compare the number of dreams remembered by each group. What do you conclude? Are dreams quickly forgotten?

7

Parapsychology: A Sixth Way to Perceive?

We normally learn about the world through our five senses: sight, hearing, touch, taste, and smell. Some people believe that many humans have a sixth sense. It is called extrasensory perception (ESP) because it does not come through any of the normal five senses. The study of the communication of ideas that does not involve one of the normal five senses is called parapsychology.

A lot of research was done on ESP by Dr. Joseph B. Rhine (1895–1980) at Duke University during the 1930s. Rhine used Zener cards to test people for ESP. A deck of Zener cards consists of 25 cards with equal numbers of five different designs (see Figure 23).

Rhine's experimental results indicated that some people have ESP. As you can see from Figure 23, if a subject simply guesses which of the five symbols is on a card, he will be right 20 percent of the time. After all, there are five choices, so the subject has one chance in five of guessing correctly. In one experiment, Rhine found a subject who was able to identify the symbol on the card held by

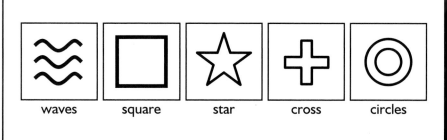

Figure 23. Zener cards carry one of these five designs. Twenty-five cards, five of each kind, make up a deck.

the experimenter nearly 40 percent of the time. The probability of obtaining such results by chance is extremely small. Rhine's results certainly indicated the existence of ESP, at least for this one person. You can carry out your own experiments for ESP and decide whether you think some people have a sixth sense.

Researchers in parapsychology claim there are three types of ESP: telepathy, clairvoyance, and precognition. Telepathy, often called mind reading, is the transfer of thoughts from one mind to another. Clairvoyance, or remote viewing, is the ability to perceive people or things from afar without using any of the five senses. Precognition is the ability to predict future events.

7-1*
Testing for Telepathy Using Zener Cards

Make a deck of Zener cards by drawing the diagrams in Figure 23 on 25 file cards (five cards for each figure). You can also use a copy machine to make five copies of the drawing. You can then glue or tape these figures to 3 inch x 5 inch file cards to make a deck of 25 cards.

Two people are needed to conduct this experiment. One person is the sender, the other is the receiver. Both know what the symbols on the cards look like.

Things you will need:

- Zener cards (deck of 25 cards) made from 3 in x 5 in file or index cards
- copier (optional)
- glue or tape (optional)
- table
- large opaque screen (You can make one from big sheet of cardboard.)
- as many people as possible
- paper
- pencil

They sit at a table on opposite sides of a big sheet of cardboard so that they cannot see one another. The sender shuffles the deck of cards and places them facedown on the table. He then removes the top card and says, "Sending" to indicate to the receiver that he is concentrating his vision and thought on a card with a particular symbol.

The receiver then tries to draw the symbol that she thinks the sender is observing. After drawing the symbol, the receiver writes 1 next to the symbol she drew to identify it as the first card. She then says, "Finished." The sender turns the first card facedown and draws a second card. The process is repeated until all 25 cards have been drawn. The receiver must be sure to number each drawing, and the sender must be sure to place the cards facedown in the order in which they were drawn.

When the sender and receiver have finished the deck, you can analyze the results. Compare, in order, the cards in the sender's deck with the numbered symbols drawn by the receiver. How many times did the symbol drawn by the receiver match the symbol on the corresponding card held by the sender? If the receiver was able to identify the card significantly more than 20 percent of the time, you should repeat the experiment with the same sender and receiver. Can he or she consistently identify the cards on which the sender is concentrating? What happens if sender and receiver reverse roles?

Try the experiment with as many people as possible. Do any of your subjects appear to have ESP?

Exploring on Your Own

Design and carry out an experiment to find out whether people can use ESP to transfer images of paintings or photographs.

Design and carry out an experiment to determine whether ESP can be used to communicate with an animal such as your pet dog or cat.

7-2*
Testing for Clairvoyance

Clairvoyance is the ability to perceive people or things from afar without using any of the normal five senses. To test for clairvoyance you will again need two people at a time, a sender and a receiver. These two people should agree that at a predetermined time the sender will be at a location unknown to the receiver. The sender will at that time concentrate on his surroundings and write a description, prepare a drawing, or take a photograph of the locale. At the same time, the receiver will prepare a written or pictorial description of the sender's location that he perceives by clairvoyance.

Things you will need:

• as many people as possible
• synchronized clocks or watches
• pens or pencils
• paper
• camera (optional)

On the next day, the two will meet with you and compare the receiver's description or drawing of the location with that of the sender. Can you detect any evidence of clairvoyance?

Repeat the experiment with as many senders and receivers as possible. Do any appear to be clairvoyant?

Exploring on Your Own

Investigate clairvoyance through books and information available at your library and on the Internet.

Read articles about clairvoyance in *Skeptical Inquirer*, a magazine published by the Committee for the Scientific Investigation of Claims of the Paranormal (CSICOP). The journalists and scientists in this organization use science to investigate the claims of paranormal activities such as clairvoyance.

7-3*
Testing for Precognition

Astrologers and psychics make predictions about future events almost daily. They predict airplane crashes, earthquakes, floods, election results, social

Things you will need:

- as many people as possible
- pencil or pen
- paper

or business success, and so on. Some of their predictions come true. However, people often ignore all the predictions that never happened and focus on the few that did. Furthermore, it is likely that predicting an airplane crash will prove to be correct because there is usually at least one airline crash each year. One would have greater confidence in such a prediction if it included the airline, the date, and the location of the crash. Such predictions are seldom made.

Predicting the outcome of an election for which the candidates have already been nominated is one in which the psychic usually has a 50:50 chance of being right; consequently, a correct prediction is not unexpected. You could probably do as well as any psychic.

To test the precognitive abilities of your friends and family, you could have them make predictions about the coming year at the beginning of a new year. You might ask them to predict the winners of each division of the American and National League baseball teams, as well as the winners of the pennants and the World Series. Ask them to make similar predictions about other professional and amateur sports, including local high school sports. Can they predict who will run for various positions in local, state, and national elections? Can they predict the winners of these elections and their margins of victory? Can they predict other events such as rainfall, hurricanes, and other weather phenomena? Be sure to let them predict any events that they themselves feel they can sense through their precognitive powers.

All these predictions should be recorded and saved. At the end of the year, review the predictions. How many hits (correct predictions) were made? Among those who made hits, what percentage of their predictions were hits? On the basis of the results, do you feel that any of your friends or members of your family have precognitive powers?

Exploring on Your Own

Obtain and read "The Book of Predictions: Fifteen Years Later," by Alan M. Tuerkheimer and Stuart A. Vyse, which can be found on pages 40–42 of the March/April 1997 issue of *Skeptical Inquirer*. What do you conclude after reading the article?

7-4*
Testing for Psychokinesis

Psychokinesis (PK) is another branch of parapsychology. It is often referred to as mind over matter. People who contend that they have psychokinetic powers claim they can change or influence physical objects without touching them. Such people might claim they can bend spoons without touching them or make bodies levitate (float in air) without lifting them. In this experiment, you can determine whether psychokinesis is a psychic ability that you possess. You will try to influence the roll of a die with your mind.

Things you will need:

• single die from a pair of dice
• plastic cup
• a friend
• pen or pencil
• notebook

Take one die from a pair of dice and put it in a small plastic cup. Before you shake the cup and roll the die out onto the floor, announce to a friend the number (1, 2, 3, 4, 5, or 6) that you are going to make come up on the top face of the die using psychokinetic powers. Assuming the die is uniform, the probability of the number you chose appearing on the die is 1:6. Therefore, your number can be expected to appear in one sixth of the rolls. If you truly have PK power, you will be able to use your mind to make the die turn up with the number you chose in significantly more than one sixth of the rolls.

To avoid biased results, your friend should read and record the number of dots on the die's top face each time you roll it. Roll the die at least 100 times.

According to chance, in what percentage of the rolls should the die's top face have the number of dots you chose? What percentage of the rolls actually showed the number you were trying to make appear by PK? Does the evidence indicate that you have PK power? If there is evidence of PK, do another 100 roles and see if there is still evidence of PK. Repeat the experiment to see if your friend has PK power. What do you find?

Exploring on Your Own

Design and carry out an experiment using the toss of a coin to test for PK. What do you find?

7-5*
Seeing Color by Touch

Some people claim they can use their sense of touch to "see" colors. You can test as many subjects as possible to find out if any of them have such mixed-up senses.

Cut squares 4 inches (10 cm) on a side from colored construction paper. Be sure all

Things you will need:

* construction paper—red, green, blue, yellow, black, and white
* scissors
* ruler
* blindfold
* as many subjects as possible

the different colored paper has the same texture. You might have red, green, blue, yellow, black, and white squares. Blindfold a subject. After making sure he cannot see, place his or her hand on one of the colored squares. Ask the subject to try to identify the color of the square. Repeat with different squares picked at random for a total of 18 trials. In how many of the trials did the subject correctly determine the color of the square? How many times might the subject pick the correct color if he or she were simply guessing?

If someone is able to correctly identify color by touch significantly more often than can be expected by guessing, check to be sure the subject is not able to see through or under the blindfold. This is the way most psychics are able to "feel" color. If you are satisfied that the subject is not peeking, continue testing until you are certain the results are not simply due to chance.

If you find someone with this uncanny ability, ask that person how he or she is able to transfer a touch sensation to a visual one. Can they explain it? Have him or her contact the Committee for the Scientific Investigation of Claims of the Paranormal (CSICOP). They publish the *Skeptical Inquirer*, and their address is Box 703, Amherst, NY 14226. The telephone number is 800-634-1610. This committee is interested in people who claim to have an ability to receive information other than through the five senses.

Exploring on Your Own

What is the neurological condition known as synesthesia?

List of Suppliers

Carolina Biological Supply Co.
2700 York Road
Burlington, NC 27215
(800) 334-5551
http://www.carolina.com

Connecticut Valley Biological Supply Co., Inc.
82 Valley Road, Box 326
Southampton, MA 01073
(800) 628-7748

Delta Education
P.O. Box 3000
Nashua, NH 03061
(800) 258-1302

Edmund Scientific Co.
60 Pearce Avenue
Tonawanda, NY 14150-6711
(800) 728-6999

Educational Innovations, Inc.
362 Main Avenue
Norwalk, CT 06851
(203) 229-0730
http://www.teachersource.com

Fisher Science Education
4500 Turnberry
Hanover Park, IL 60133
(800) 955-1177
http://www.fisheredu.com

Frey Scientific
100 Paragon Parkway
Mansfield, OH 44903
(800) 225-3739

NASCO-Modesto
4825 Stoddard Road
Modesto, CA 95352-3837
(800) 558-9595
http://www.nascofa.com

Nasco-Fort Atkinson
P.O. Box 901
Fort Atkinson, WI 53538-0901
(800) 558-9595

Sargent-Welch/VWR Scientific
P.O. Box 5229
Buffalo Grove, IL 60089-5229
(800) SAR-GENT
http://www.sargentwelch.com

Science Kit & Boreal Laboratories
P.O. Box 5003
Tonawanda, NY 14150-5003
(800) 828-7777
http://sciencekit.com

Ward's Natural Science Establishment, Inc.
P.O. Box 92912
Rochester, NY 14692-9012
(800) 962-2660
http://www.wardsci.com

Further Reading

Baines, Gwendolyn L. *People in the Web of Life. 2nd Edition.* Nashville, Tenn.: Nevada Publishing Company, 1992.

Gardner, Robert. *Health Science Projects About Anatomy and Physiology.* Berkeley Heights, N.J.: Enslow Publishers, Inc., 2001.

———. *Health Science Projects About Your Senses.* Berkeley Heights, N.J.: Enslow Publishers, Inc., 2001.

———. *What's So Super About the Supernatural?* Brookfield, Conn.: Twenty-First Century Books, 1998.

Kincher, Jonni. *Psychology for Kids: 40 Fun Tests That Help You Learn About Yourself.* Minneapolis: Free Spirit Publishing, 1995.

———. *Psychology for Kids II: 40 Fun Experiments That Help You Learn About Others.* Minneapolis: Free Spirit Publishing, 1995.

Internet Addresses

Committee for the Scientific Investigation of Claims of the
  Paranormal (CSICOP).
    <http://www.csicop.org>.

Franklin Institute Science Museum.
    <http://sln.fi.edu>.

Forsyth's Overview of Psychology.
    <http://www.has.vcu.edu/psy/psy101/forsyth/psych.htm>.

Guide to Doing Science Projects.
    <http://www.isd77.k12.mn.us/resources/cf/SciProjIntro.html>.

Human Anatomy and Physiology.
    <http://www.dmnh.org/hol_prgm.htm>.

The WWW Virtual Library: Science Fairs.
    <http://physics.usc.edu/~gould/ScienceFairs/>.

Index